Careers in Focus

BIOLOGY

SECOND EDITION

Ferguson
An imprint of ☑®Facts On File

Careers in Focus: Biology, Second Edition

Copyright © 2006 by Facts On File, Inc.

Ferguson
An imprint of Facts On File, Inc.
132 West 31st Street
New York NY 10001

Library of Congress Cataloging-in-Publication Data
Careers in focus. Biology—2nd ed.
   p.   cm.
   Includes index.
   ISBN 0-8160-5867-9 (hc: alk. paper)
   1. Biology—Vocational guidance—Juvenile literature. I. Title: Biology. II. J.G. Ferguson Publishing Company.
   QH314.C37 2005
   570'.23—dc22   2005014965

Ferguson books are available at special discounts when purchased in bulk quantities for businesses, associations, institutions, or sales promotions. Please call our Special Sales Department in New York at (212) 967-8800 or (800) 322-8755.

You can find Ferguson on the World Wide Web at http://www.fergpubco.com

Text design by David Strelecky

Printed in the United States of America

MP JT 10 9 8 7 6 5 4 3 2 1

This book is printed on acid-free paper.

Table of Contents

Introduction

Biology subfields are many and varied and include microbiology, plant and animal physiology, ecology, epidemiology, cell biology, and oceanography, just to name a few. For all these areas, the elements of the job are essentially the same: building on the work of others, both past and present, through experimentation and observation.

Most research in biology uses a team approach. Team members review previous research and experiments and then set a goal for their project. They may either form a hypothesis (an educated guess) to prove or disprove a current theory, or they may set an open-ended objective, such as finding out what happens over time to people who smoke or drink. An experiment may prove something, or it may not. After experimentation, the biologist analyzes the results, often publishing his or her findings in a scientific journal article. Publishing results is a key part of doing research, for only by sharing data and evaluations can the scientific community make the most of research. Scientists working under contracts with research companies do not own their discoveries: Their research becomes the property of their employer. Scientists working independently can keep their discoveries as their own and have the right to patent and charge others for using their research.

Generally, those working in the biology field do one of four types of work: basic research, applied research, testing, or support. Basic research seeks knowledge for its own sake, uncovering fundamental truths and transforming the unknown into the known. Often done at universities, basic research includes all areas of biology. Applied research deals with translating basic knowledge into practical and useful products and processes for use in areas such as medicine or agriculture.

Research biologists at universities generally split their time between their research projects and teaching. High school teachers often specialize in biology and may teach courses that interest them personally, such as marine biology or physiology. Because researchers need skilled help from others trained in biology, some biologists work in support roles, such as laboratory technicians, who help carry out experiments. All specialists must combine a thorough knowledge of general biology with other skills and professional training.

Many people in the biology field do work that combines their knowledge of biology with other specialized training. The "office" for many of these jobs is the outdoors, and dress is casual. Zookeepers, for example, may work with captive breeding programs for endangered species. Zoos, museums, and nature centers hire educators, exhibit designers, artists, and other specialists with biology backgrounds. Those with a talent for writing may work as science journalists, breaking down science so that nonexperts can understand the concepts. Other biologists work as policy analysts in government, helping to develop science-based legislation. Physicians, dentists, nurses, medical technicians, and physician assistants must also have solid biology backgrounds.

The U.S. Department of Labor predicts average job growth in the biology field over the next decade. However, biological scientists with Ph.D.'s may face stiff competition for research positions due to an increased number of doctorate-level biologists competing for the research grants. Although the federal government has substantially increased the amounts and kinds of grants available for biological research, only about 1 in 3 research proposals are approved for long-term studies, which reflects the strong competition in this field. Job opportunities for biologists with bachelor's and master's degrees will be better, as available positions in biology-related sales, marketing, education, and research management positions should be plentiful. The demand for biology-related technician positions in medicine and technology that do not require advanced degrees is also expected to be high. Continued and expanded research into diseases such as AIDS, cancer, and Alzheimer's and the need to develop new drugs and therapies to combat these diseases will also provide many opportunities for employment in the biology field.

Some of the articles in *Careers in Focus: Biology* appear in Ferguson's *Encyclopedia of Careers and Vocational Guidance*, but they have been updated and revised with the latest information from the U.S. Department of Labor, professional organizations, and other sources. In addition, this revised edition of the book includes new articles on ethnoscientists and veterinarians.

The **Quick Facts** section provides a brief summary of the career including recommended school subjects, personal skills, work environment, minimum educational requirements, salary ranges, certification or licensing requirements, and employment outlook. This section also provides acronyms and identification numbers for the following government classification indexes: the *Dictionary of Occupational Titles* (DOT), the *Guide for Occupational Exploration* (GOE), the National Occupational Classification (NOC) Index, and the Occupational Information Network (O*NET)-Standard Occupational Classification System (SOC) index. The DOT, GOE, and O*NET-SOC indexes have been created by the U.S. government;

the NOC index is Canada's career classification system. Readers can use the identification numbers listed in the Quick Facts section to access further information about a career. Print editions of the DOT (*Dictionary of Occupational Titles*. Indianapolis, Ind.: JIST Works, 1991) and GOE (*The Guide for Occupational Exploration*. 3d ed. Indianapolis, Ind.: JIST Works, 2001) are available at libraries. Electronic versions of the NOC (http://www23.hrdc-drhc.gc.ca) and O*NET-SOC (http://online.onetcenter.org) are available on the World Wide Web. When no DOT, GOE, NOC, or O*NET-SOC numbers are present, this means that the U.S. Department of Labor or Human Resources Development Canada have not created a numerical designation for this career. In this instance, you will see the acronym "N/A," or not available.

The **Overview** section is a brief introductory description of the duties and responsibilities involved in this career. A career may have a variety of associated job titles. When this is the case, alternative career titles are presented.

The **History** section describes the history of the particular job as it relates to the overall development of its industry or field.

The Job describes the primary and secondary duties of the job.

Requirements discusses high school and postsecondary education and training requirements, any certification or licensing that is necessary, and other personal requirements for success in the job.

Exploring offers suggestions on how to gain experience in or knowledge of the particular job before making a firm educational and financial commitment. The focus is on what can be done while still in high school (or in the early years of college) to gain a better understanding of the job.

The **Employers** section gives an overview of typical places of employment for the job.

Starting Out discusses the best ways to land that first job, be it through the college placement office, newspaper ads, or personal contact.

The **Advancement** section describes what kind of career path to expect from the job and how to get there.

Earnings lists salary ranges and describes the typical fringe benefits.

The **Work Environment** section describes the typical surroundings and conditions of employment—whether indoors or outdoors, noisy or quiet, social or independent. Also discussed are typical hours worked, any seasonal fluctuations, and the stresses and strains of the job.

The **Outlook** section summarizes the job in terms of the general economy and industry projections. For the most part, Outlook information is obtained from the U.S. Bureau of Labor Statistics and is supplemented by information taken from professional associations. Job growth terms follow those used in the *Occupational Outlook Handbook*. Growth described as "much faster than the average" means an increase of 36 percent or more. Growth described as "faster than the average" means an increase of 21 to 35 percent. Growth described as "about as fast as the average" means an increase of 10 to 20 percent. Growth described as "more slowly than the average" means an increase of 3 to 9 percent. Growth described as "little or no change" means an increase of 0 to 2 percent. "Decline" means a decrease of 1 percent or more.

Each article ends with **For More Information,** which lists organizations that provide information on training, education, internships, scholarships, and job placement.

Careers in Focus: Biology also includes photos, informative sidebars, and interviews with professionals in the field.

Agricultural Scientists

OVERVIEW

Agricultural scientists study all aspects of living organisms and the relationships of plants and animals to their environment. They conduct basic research in laboratories or in the field. They apply the results to such tasks as increasing crop yields and improving the environment. Some agricultural scientists plan and administer programs for testing foods, drugs, and other products. Others direct activities at public exhibits at such places as zoos and botanical gardens. Some agricultural scientists are professors at colleges and universities or work as consultants to business firms or the government. Others work in technical sales and service jobs for manufacturers of agricultural products. There are approximately 18,000 agricultural and food scientists in the United States; about 40 percent work for the federal, state, or local governments. Several thousand more are employed as university professors.

HISTORY

In 1840, Justius von Liebig of Germany published *Organic Chemistry in Its Applications to Agriculture and Physiology* and launched the systematic development of the agricultural sciences. A formal system of agricultural education soon followed in both Europe and the United States. Prior to the publication of this work, agricultural developments relied on the collective experience of farmers handed down over generations. Agricultural science has techniques in common with many other disciplines including biology, botany, genetics, nutrition, breeding, and

QUICK FACTS

School Subjects
Biology
Chemistry

Personal Skills
Communication/ideas
Technical/scientific

Work Environment
Indoors and outdoors
Primarily multiple locations

Minimum Education Level
Bachelor's degree

Salary Range
$28,750 to $49,610 to
$86,930+

Certification or Licensing
Voluntary (certification)
Required for certain
positions (licensing)

Outlook
Little change or more slowly
than the average

DOT
040

GOE
02.07.01

NOC
2121

O*NET-SOC
17-2021.00, 19-1011.00,
19-1013.01

engineering. Discoveries and improvements in these fields contributed to advances in agriculture. Some milestones include the discovery of the practice of crop rotation and the application of manure as fertilizer, which greatly increased farm yields in the 1700s. Farm mechanization was greatly advanced by the invention of the mechanical reaper in 1831 and the gasoline tractor in 1892. Chemical fertilizers were first used in the 19th century; pesticides and herbicides soon followed. In 1900, the research of an Austrian monk, Gregor Johann Mendel, was rediscovered. His theories of plant characteristics, based on studies using generations of garden peas, formed the foundation for the science of genetics.

In the 20th century, scientists and engineers were at the forefront of farm, crop, and food processing improvements. Conservationist Gifford Pinchot developed some of the first methods to prevent soil erosion in 1910, and Clarence Birdseye perfected a method of freezing food in the 1920s. Birdseye's discoveries allowed for new crops of produce previously too perishable for the marketplace. Engineers in the 1930s developed more powerful farm machinery and scientists developed hybrid corn. By the 1960s, high-powered machinery and better quality feed and pesticides were in common use. Today, advances in genetic engineering and biotechnology are leading to more efficient, economical methods of farming and new markets for crops.

THE JOB

The nature of the work of the agricultural scientist can be broken down into several areas of specialization. Within each specialization there are various careers.

The following are careers that fall under the areas of plant and soil science.

Agronomists investigate large-scale food-crop problems, conduct experiments, and develop new methods of growing crops to ensure more efficient production, higher yields, and improved quality. They use genetic engineering to develop crops that are resistant to pests, drought, and plant diseases.

Agronomists also engage in soil science. They analyze soils to find ways to increase production and reduce soil erosion. They study the responses of various soil types to fertilizers, tillage practices, and crop rotation. Since soil science is related to environmental science, agronomists may also use their expertise to consult with farmers and agricultural companies on environmental quality and effective land use.

Agricultural Research Service (ARS) plant pathologist Scott Abney (left) and research assistant Tom Richards check the growth of soybeans inoculated with field isolates of *Phytophthors sojae. (Photo by Scott Bauer/USDA)*

Botanists are concerned with plants and their environment, structure, heredity, and economic value in such fields as agronomy, horticulture, and medicine.

Horticulturists study fruit and nut orchards as well as garden plants such as vegetables and flowers. They conduct experiments to develop new and improved varieties and to increase crop quality and yields. They also work to improve plant culture methods for the landscaping and beautification of communities, parks, and homes.

Plant breeders apply the principles of genetics and biotechnology to improve plants' yield, quality, and resistance to harsh weather, disease, and insects. They might work on developing strains of wild or cultivated plants that will have a larger yield and increase profits.

Plant pathologists research plant diseases and the decay of plant products to identify symptoms, determine causes, and develop control measures. They attempt to predict outbreaks by studying how different soils, climates, and geography affect the spread and intensity of plant disease.

Another area of specialization for agricultural scientists is animal science.

Animal scientists conduct research and develop improved methods for housing, breeding, feeding, and controlling diseases of domestic farm animals. They inspect and grade livestock food products, purchase livestock, or work in sales and marketing of livestock products. They often consult agricultural businesses on such areas as upgrading animal housing, lowering mortality rates, or increasing production of animal products such as milk and eggs.

Dairy scientists study the selection, breeding, feeding, and management of dairy cattle. For example, they research how various types of food and environmental conditions affect milk production and quality. They also develop new breeding programs to improve dairy herds.

Poultry scientists study the breeding, feeding, and management of poultry to improve the quantity and quality of eggs and other poultry products.

Animal breeders specialize in improving the quality of farm animals. They may work for a state agricultural department, agricultural extension station, or university. Some of their work is done in a laboratory, but much of it is done outdoors working directly on animals. Using their knowledge of genetics, animal breeders develop systems for animals to achieve desired characteristics such as strength, fast maturation, resistance to disease, and quality of meat.

Food science is a specialty closely related to animal science, but it focuses on meeting consumer demand for food products in ways that are healthy, safe, and convenient.

Food scientists use their backgrounds in chemistry, microbiology, and other sciences to develop new or better ways of preserving, packaging, processing, storing, and delivering foods. *Food technologists* work in product development to discover new food sources and ana-

Beyond the Laboratory

Agricultural science isn't limited to food, plant, soil, and animal science. Many scientists are also concerned with range lands and pastures, and with grazing management. According to the USDA, one-half of the Earth's land surface is grazed. Fifty-five percent of U.S. land surface is made up of range lands, pastures, and hay lands. U.S. hay production amounts to $11 billion a year, and grazing lands support a livestock industry that contributes $78 billion a year in farm sales to the U.S. economy.

lyze food content to determine levels of vitamins, fat, sugar, and protein. Food technologists also work to enforce government regulations, inspecting food processing areas and ensuring that sanitation, safety, quality, and waste management standards are met.

Another field related to agricultural science is agricultural engineering.

Agricultural engineers apply engineering principles to work in the food and agriculture industries. They design or develop agricultural equipment and machines, supervise production, and conduct tests on new designs and machine parts. They develop plans and specifications for agricultural buildings and for drainage and irrigation systems. They work on flood control, soil erosion, and land reclamation projects. They design food processing systems and equipment to convert farm products to consumer foods. Agricultural engineers contribute to making farming easier and more profitable through the introduction of new farm machinery and through advancements in soil and water conservation. Agricultural engineers in industry engage in research or in the design, testing, or sales of equipment.

Much of the research conducted by agricultural scientists is done in laboratories and requires a familiarity with research techniques and the use of laboratory equipment and computers. Some research, however, is carried out wherever necessary. A botanist may have occasion to examine the plants that grow in the volcanic valleys of Alaska, or an animal breeder may study the behavior of animals on the plains of Africa.

REQUIREMENTS

High School

Follow your high school's college preparatory program, which will include courses in English, foreign language, mathematics, and government. Also take biology, chemistry, physics, and any other science courses available. You must also become familiar with basic computer skills, including programming. It may be possible for you to perform laboratory assistant duties for your science teachers. Visiting research laboratories and attending lectures by agricultural scientists can also be helpful.

Postsecondary Training

Educational requirements for agricultural scientists are very high. A doctorate is usually mandatory for careers as college or university professors, independent researchers, or field managers. A bachelor's degree may be acceptable for some entry-level jobs, such as testing or inspecting technicians, or as technical sales or service representatives. Promotions, however, are very limited for these employees unless they earn advanced degrees.

To become an agricultural scientist, you should pursue a degree related to agricultural and biological science. As an undergraduate, you should have a firm foundation in biology, with courses in chemistry, physics, mathematics, and English. Most colleges and universities have agricultural science curriculums, although liberal arts colleges may emphasize the biological sciences. State universities usually offer agricultural science programs, too.

While pursuing an advanced degree, you'll participate in research projects and write a dissertation on your specialized area of study. You'll also do fieldwork and laboratory research along with your classroom studies.

Certification or Licensing

A voluntary certification program is offered by the Federation of Certifying Boards in Agriculture, Biology, Earth and Environmental Sciences, which was originally known as American Registry of Certified Professionals in Agronomy, Crops and Soils (ARCPACS). The federation, however, still uses the acronym ARCPACS, and it is associated with the American Society of Argonomy. ARCPACS offers a number of certifications, such as certified professional agronomist (CPA) and certified professional plant pathologist (CPPP), to candidates based on their training and work. In general, requirements include meeting a minimum education level and having a certain amount of work experience (for example, a bachelor's degree and five years of work experience or a master's degree and three years of experience), passing an exam, and having appropriate references. Recertification requirements typically include the completion of a certain amount of continuing education credits every two years in addition to payment of dues and adherence to a code of ethics.

According to the American Society of Agricultural Engineers, agricultural engineers must hold an engineer's license.

Other Requirements

As a researcher, you should be self-motivated enough to work alone, yet be able to function cooperatively as part of a team. You should have an inexhaustible curiosity about the nature of living things and their environments. You must be systematic in your work habits and in your approach to investigation and experimentation and must have the persistence to continue or start over when experiments are not immediately successful.

Work performed by agricultural scientists in offices and laboratories requires intense powers of concentration and the ability to communicate one's thoughts systematically. In addition to these skills, physical stamina is necessary for those scientists who do field research in remote areas of the world.

EXPLORING

If you live in an agricultural community, you may be able to find part-time or summer work on a farm or ranch. Joining a chapter of the National FFA Organization (formerly Future Farmers of America) or a 4-H program will introduce you to the concerns of farmers and researchers and may involve you directly in science projects. Contact your county's extension office to learn about regional projects. You may also find part-time work in veterinarians' offices, florist shops, landscape nurseries, orchards, farms, zoos, aquariums, botanical gardens, or museums. Volunteer work is often available in zoos and animal shelters.

EMPLOYERS

About 40 percent of all agricultural scientists work for federal, state, and local governments. They work within the U.S. Department of Agriculture and the Environmental Protection Agency and for regional extension agencies and soil conservation departments. Scientists with doctorates may work on the faculty of colleges and universities. Researchers work for chemical and pharmaceutical companies, and with agribusiness and consulting firms. Agricultural scientists also work in the food processing industry.

STARTING OUT

Agricultural scientists often are recruited prior to graduation. College and university placement offices offer information about jobs, and students may arrange interviews with recruiters who visit the campus.

Direct application may be made to the personnel departments of colleges and universities, private industries, and nonprofit research foundations. People interested in positions with the federal government may contact the local offices of state employment services and the U.S. Office of Personnel Management or the Federal Job Information Centers, which are located in various large cities throughout the country. Private employment agencies are another method that might be considered. Large companies sometimes conduct job fairs in major cities and will advertise them in the business sections of the local newspapers.

ADVANCEMENT

Advancement in this field depends on education, experience, and job performance. Agricultural scientists with advanced degrees generally start in teaching or research and advance to administrative and management positions, such as supervisor of a research program. The number of such jobs is limited, however, and often the route to advancement is through specialization. The narrower specialties are often the most valuable.

People who enter this field with only a bachelor's degree are much more restricted. After starting in testing and inspecting jobs or as technical sales and service representatives, they may progress to advanced technicians, particularly in medical research, or become high school biology teachers. In the latter case, they must have had courses in education and meet the state requirements for teaching credentials.

EARNINGS

According to the U.S. Department of Labor, the median annual salary of agricultural and food scientists (from all specialty areas) was approximately $49,610 in 2003. The lowest paid 10 percent (which generally included those just starting out in the field) earned less than $29,250, while the highest paid 10 percent made approximately $86,930 or more per year. Agricultural scientists working for the federal government earned the highest average salaries in the field: $65,450 a year.

Unless hired for just a short-term project, agricultural scientists most likely receive health and retirement benefits in addition to their annual salary.

WORK ENVIRONMENT

Agricultural scientists work regular hours, although researchers often choose to work longer when their experiments have reached critical points. Competition in the research field may be stiff, causing a certain amount of stress.

Agricultural scientists generally work in offices, laboratories, or classrooms where the environment is clean, healthy, and safe. Some agricultural scientists, such as botanists, periodically take field trips where living facilities may be primitive and strenuous physical activity may be required.

OUTLOOK

According to the U.S. Department of Labor, employment for agricultural scientists is expected to grow more slowly than the average through 2012. This reflects a slowdown in government employment as well as in private industry, though the field as a whole is less vulnerable to recession than many other occupations. Despite slower growth, retirees and others who leave agricultural science will still need to be replaced.

The fields of biotechnology, genetics, and sustainable agriculture may hold the best opportunities for agricultural scientists. New developments, such as methods of processing corn for use in medicines, will alter the marketplace. Scientists will also be actively involved in improving both the environmental impact of farming and crop yields, as they focus on methods of decontaminating soil, protecting groundwater, crop rotation, and other efforts of conservation. Scientists will also have the challenge of promoting these new methods to farmers.

FOR MORE INFORMATION

To learn about opportunities for scientists in the dairy industry and for information on student divisions at the college level, contact
American Dairy Science Association
1111 North Dunlap Avenue
Savoy, IL 61874
Tel: 217-356-5146
Email: adsa@assochq.org
http://www.adsa.org

To learn about student competitions and scholarships, contact
American Society of Agricultural Engineers
2950 Niles Road
St. Joseph, MI 49085
Tel: 269-429-0300
http://www.asae.org

For the career resource guide Exploring Careers in Agronomy, Crops, Soils, and Environmental Sciences, *and certification information, contact*
American Society of Agronomy
677 South Segoe Road
Madison, WI 53711
Tel: 608-273-8080
http://www.agronomy.org

For more information on agricultural careers and student programs, contact
National FFA Organization
PO Box 68960
6060 FFA Drive
Indianapolis, IN 46268
Tel: 317-802-6060
http://www.ffa.org

Visit the USDA website for more information on its agencies and programs as well as news releases.
United States Department of Agriculture (USDA)
http://www.usda.gov

Aquarists

OVERVIEW

Aquarists (pronounced, like "aquarium," with the accent on the second syllable) work for aquariums, oceanariums, and marine research institutes. They are responsible for the maintenance of aquatic exhibits. Among other duties, they feed the fish, check water quality, clean the tanks, and collect and transport new specimens.

HISTORY

In 1853, the world's first public aquarium opened in Regents Park in London. Similar public aquariums opened throughout England, France, and Germany over the next 15 years. Many of the early aquariums closed because the fish could not survive in the conditions provided. By the early 1870s, knowledge of aeration, filtering, and water temperature had increased, and new aquariums opened.

In 1856, the U.S. government established what is today the Division of Fishes of the Smithsonian Institution's National Museum of Natural History. Over the next 50 years interest in fish and their environments grew rapidly. The Woods Hole Oceanographic Institute was established in 1885, and the Scripps Institution of Oceanography was established in 1903.

Today's notable aquariums include the John G. Shedd Aquarium, Chicago; the National Aquarium, Baltimore; the New York Aquarium, New York City; the Steinhart Aquarium, San Francisco; and the Aquarium of the Americas, New Orleans. Many aquariums recreate diverse aquatic environments, such as coral reefs, river bottoms, or various coastlines, in large tanks.

Some aquariums also have oceanariums—huge tanks that allow visitors to view marine animals from above as well as from the sides. Popular oceanariums include those at the Miami Seaquarium in Miami, Florida, and the Monterey Bay Aquarium in Monterey, California.

THE JOB

Aquarists (pronounced, like "aquarium," with the accent on the second syllable) work for aquariums, oceanariums, and marine research institutes. Aquarists are not animal trainers and do not work on marine shows. They do, however, support the staff who do. Their work is generally technical and requires a strong science background. With increased experience and education, aquarists may, in time, become involved in research efforts at their institution or become promoted to higher professional positions such as curator.

Aquarists' job duties are similar to those of zookeepers. Aquarists feed fish, maintain exhibits, and conduct research. They work on breeding, conservation, and educational programs.

Aquarists clean and take care of tanks every day. They make sure pumps are working, check water temperatures, clean glass, and sift sand. Some exhibits have to be scrubbed by hand. Aquarists also change the water and vacuum tanks routinely. They water plants in marsh or pond exhibits.

Food preparation and feeding are important tasks for aquarists. Some animals eat live food and others eat cut-up food mixtures. Some animals need special diets prepared and may have to be individually fed.

Aquarists carefully observe all the animals in their care. They must understand their normal habits (including mating, feeding, sleeping, and moving) in order to be able to judge when something is wrong. Aquarists write daily reports and keep detailed records of animal behavior.

Many aquarists are in charge of collecting and stocking plants and animals for exhibits. They may have to make several trips a year to gather live specimens.

REQUIREMENTS

High School

If you want to become an aquarist, get your start in high school. Take as many science classes as you can; biology and zoology are especially important. Learn to pay attention to detail; marine science involves a good deal of careful record keeping.

Books to Read

Boruchowitz, David. *The Simple Guide to Fresh Water Aquariums.* Neptune, N.J.: TFH Publications, 2001.

Calfo, Anthony, and Robert Fenner. *Reef Invertebrates: An Essential Guide to Selection, Care, and Compatibility.* Monroeville, Pa.: Reading Trees, 2003.

Dakin, Nick. *Complete Encyclopedia of the Saltwater Aquarium.* Firefly Books, 2003.

Michael, Scott W. *Marine Fishes: 500+ Essential-to-Know Aquarium Species.* Neptune, N.J.: TFH Publications, 1999.

Mills, Dick. *101 Essential Tips: Aquarium Fish.* New York: DK Publishing, 1996.

Tullock, John H. *Water Chemistry for the Marine Aquarium.* Happauge, N.Y.: Barron's, 2002.

Postsecondary Training

Most aquariums, along with other institutions that hire aquarists, require that an applicant have a bachelor's degree in biological sciences, preferably with course work in such areas as parasitology, ichthyology, or other aquatic sciences. As the care of captive animals becomes a more complex discipline, it's no longer enough to apply without a four-year degree.

Certification or Licensing

Aquarists must be able to scuba dive, in both contained water, to feed fish and maintain tanks, and in open water, on trips to collect new specimens. You'll need to have scuba certification, with a rescue diver classification, for this job. Potential employers will expect you to be able to pass a diving physical examination before taking you on as an aquarist.

Other Requirements

As an aquarist, you may be required to travel at different times throughout the year, to participate in research expeditions and collecting trips. On a more basic level, aquarists need to be in good physical shape, with good hearing and visual acuity. Some employers also require a certain strength level—say, the ability to regularly exert 100 pounds of force—since equipment, feed, and the animals themselves can be heavy and often unwieldy.

EXPLORING

In addition to formal education, many aquariums, like other types of museums, look for a strong interest in the field before hiring an applicant. Most often, they look for a history of volunteering. That means you need to look for every avenue you can find to work around fish or other animals. Do as much as your schedule allows. Even working part-time or volunteering at a local pet store counts. Also, be sure to ask your career guidance counselor for information on marine science careers and opportunities for summer internships or college scholarships offered by larger institutes.

EMPLOYERS

Aquarists most often work in zoos, public aquariums, or in research jobs with marine science institutes.

STARTING OUT

Full-time jobs for aquarists can be scarce, especially for those just starting in the field. Part-time or volunteer positions with zoos, aquariums, science institutes, nature centers, or even pet stores could provide valuable preliminary experience that may eventually lead to a full-time position.

ADVANCEMENT

The usual career path for an aquarist progresses from intern/volunteer through part-time work to full-fledged aquarist, senior aquarist, supervisor, and finally, curator. Each step along the path requires additional experience and often additional education. Curators generally are expected to have a Ph.D. in a relevant marine science discipline, for example. The career path of an aquarist depends on how much hands-on work they like to do with animals. Other options are available for aquarists who are looking for a less "down and dirty" experience.

EARNINGS

Aquariums often are nonprofit institutions, limiting the earnings ability in this job somewhat. In general, aquarists make between $23,000 and $32,000 a year, or between about $11 and $15 per hour. Aquariums do offer fairly extensive benefits, however, including health insurance, 401(k) plans, continuing education opportunities, tuition reimbursement, and reciprocal benefits with many other cultural institutions.

WORK ENVIRONMENT

Aquarists may work indoors or outdoors, depending on the facility for which they work and the exhibit to which they're assigned. Aquarists spend a lot of time in the water. Their day will be filled with a variety of tasks, some repetitive, like feeding, others unusual, such as working with rescued marine mammals, perhaps. In the beginning, aquarists work under the supervision of a senior aquarist or supervisor and may work as part of a team. Aquarists also can expect to travel as part of the job.

OUTLOOK

There is, in general, little change in the availability of positions for aquarists. While terrestrial zoos have begun to add aquarium complexes to their campuses in growing numbers, an actual boom in the construction of new aquariums is unlikely at this time. Many aquarists do advance to other positions, however, so openings do become available.

FOR MORE INFORMATION

For information on careers in aquatic and marine science, including job listings, contact
American Zoo and Aquarium Association
8403 Colesville Road, Suite 710
Silver Spring, MD 20910-3314
Tel: 301-562-0777
Email: generalinquiry@aza.org
http://www.aza.org

For information on guided tours and other opportunities, contact
Columbus Zoo and Aquarium
9990 Riverside Drive
Powell, OH 43065
Tel: 614-645-3550
http://www.colszoo.org

For information on educational programs, summer internships, and courses, contact the following organizations:

Marine Science Center
Northeastern University
430 Nahant Road
Nahant, MA 01908
Tel: 781-581-7370
http://www.marinescience.neu.edu

Marine Science Institute
500 Discovery Parkway
Redwood City, CA 94063-4715
Tel: 650-364-2760
Email: info@sfbaymsi.org
http://www.sfbaymsi.org

Marine Science Institute
University of Texas at Austin
750 Channel View Drive
Port Aransas, TX 78373-5015
Tel: 361-749-6711
http://www.utmsi.utexas.edu

Arborists

OVERVIEW

Arborists are professionals who practice arboriculture, which is the care of trees and shrubs, especially those found in urban areas. Arborists prune and fertilize trees and other woody plants as well as monitor them for insects and diseases. Arborists are often consulted for various tree-related issues.

HISTORY

Arboriculture developed as a branch of the plant science of horticulture. While related to the study of forestry, arborists view their specimens on an individual level; foresters manage trees as a group.

Trees are important to our environment. Besides releasing oxygen back to our atmosphere, trees enrich our soil with their fallen, decaying leaves, and their roots aid in the prevention of soil erosion. Trees provide shelter and a source of food for many different types of animals. People use trees as ornamentation. Trees are often planted to protect against the wind and glare of the sun, block offensive views, mark property lines, and provide privacy. Trees and shrubs often add considerably to a home's property value.

All trees need proper care and seasonal maintenance. The occupation of *tree surgeon,* as arborists were first known, came from the need for qualified individuals to care for trees and shrubs, as well as woody vines and ground-cover plants. Trees planted in busy city areas and in the suburbs face pollution, traffic, crowding, extreme temperatures, and other daily hazards. City trees often have a large percentage of their roots covered with concrete. Roots of larger trees sometimes interfere with plumbing pipes, sidewalks, and building foundations.

Branches can interfere with buildings or power lines. Trees located along the sides of roads and highways must be maintained; branches are pruned, and fallen leaves and fruit are gathered. Proper intervention, if not prevention, of diseases is an important task of arborists.

THE JOB

Trees and shrubs need more than just sunlight and water. That's where arborists take over. Arborists perform many different tasks for trees and shrubs, some for the sake of maintenance and others for the tree's health and well-being.

Pruning. All trees need some amount of pruning to control their shape; sometimes limbs are trimmed if they interfere with power lines, if they cross property lines, or if they grow too close to houses and other buildings. Arborists may use tools such as pruning shears or hand and power saws to do the actual cutting. If the branches are especially large or cumbersome, arborists may rope them together before the sawing begins. After cutting, the branches can be safely lowered to the ground. Ladders, aerial lifts, and cranes may be used to reach extremely tall trees. Sometimes, arborists need to cable or brace tree limbs weakened by disease or old age or damaged by a storm.

Planting or transplanting. When cities or towns plan a new development, or wish to gentrify an existing one, they often consult with arborists to determine what types of trees to plant. Arborists can suggest trees that will thrive in a certain environment. Young plantings, or immature trees, are more cost effective and are often used, though sometimes, larger, more mature trees are transplanted to the desired location.

Diagnosis and treatment. A large part of keeping a tree healthy is the prevention of disease. There are a number of diseases that affect trees, among them anthracnose and Dutch elm disease. Insects pose a potential threat to trees, and have done considerable damage to certain species in the past, by boring into the trunk or spreading disease-causing organisms. Bacteria, fungi, viruses, and disease-causing organisms can also be fatal enemies of trees. Arborists are specially trained to identify the insect or the disease weakening the tree and apply the necessary remedy or medication. Common methods prescribed by arborists include chemical insecticides, or the use of natural insect predators to combat the problem. Arborists closely monitor insect migrations or any other situations that may be harmful to a species of tree.

When a tree is too old or badly diseased, arborists may choose to cut it down. Arborists will carefully cut the tree into pieces to prevent injury to people or damage to surrounding property.

Prevention. Trees, especially young plantings, often need extra nourishment. Arborists are trained to apply fertilizers, both natural and chemical, in a safe and environmentally friendly manner. Arborists are also hired by golf courses and parks to install lightning protection systems for lone trees or mature, valuable trees.

REQUIREMENTS

High School
High school biology classes can provide you with a solid background to be a successful arborist. An interest in gardening, conservation, or the outdoors is also helpful.

Postsecondary Training
Take classes in botany, chemistry, horticulture, and plant pathology. Several colleges and universities offer programs in arboriculture and other related fields such as landscape design, nursery stock production, or grounds and turf maintenance. Entry-level positions such as assistants or climbers do not need a college degree for employment. Advanced education, however, is highly desired if you plan to make this field your career.

Certification or Licensing
The National Arborist Association (NAA) and the International Society of Arboriculture (ISA) both offer various home study courses and books on arboriculture. Most arborists are certified or licensed. Licensure ensures an arborist meets the state's regulations for working with pesticides and herbicides. Check with your local government—not all states require arborists to be licensed. Certification, given by the ISA after completion of required training and education, is considered by many as a measure of an arborist's skill and experience in the industry. Today's savvy consumers specifically look for certified arborists when it comes to caring for their trees and other precious landscaping plants. Arborists need to apply for recertification every three years and must complete 30 units of continuing education classes and seminars.

EXPLORING

Interested in this field? Surfing the Internet can provide a wealth of information for you to browse. Log onto the websites of the NAA or

ISA for industry and career information. If you really want to test the waters, why not find summer work with an arborist? You'll earn extra spending money while at the same learning about the industry firsthand. Check with the NAA for a complete listing of certified arborists in your area.

EMPLOYERS

Landscaping companies and businesses that offer a host of expert tree services are common employers of arborists. Employment opportunities are also available with municipal governments, botanical gardens, and arboretums. For example, an arborist in the Chicago area may want to seek a position with the Chicago Botanic Gardens or the Morton Arboretum; both places are known for their lush gardens and wooded trails. According to the Department of Labor, there were about 59,000 arborists in the United States in 2002.

STARTING OUT

So you've decided to become an arborist—what's the next step? Start by compiling a list of tree care firms in your area, then send your resume or fill out an application to the companies that interest you. You should also consider employment with the highway or park department of your city or county—they often hire crews to maintain their trees.

Many colleges and universities offer job placement services and post employment opportunities in their career offices. Industry associations and trade magazines are often good sources of job openings.

Don't plan to climb to the top of an American elm your first day on the job. Expect to stay at ground level, at least for a few days. Trainees in this industry start as *helpers* or *ground workers,* who load and unload equipment from trucks, gather branches and other debris for disposal, handle ropes, and give assistance to climbers. They also operate the chipper—a machine that cuts large branches into small chips. After some time observing more experienced workers, trainees are allowed to climb smaller trees or the lower limbs of large trees. They are also taught the proper way to operate large machinery and climbing gear. Most companies provide on-the-job training that lasts from one to three months.

ADVANCEMENT

Experienced arborists can advance to supervisory positions such as crew manager or department supervisor. Another option is to become a consultant in the field and work for tree care firms, city or town boards, large nurseries, or gardening groups.

Arborists with a strong entrepreneurial nature can choose to open their own business, but aspiring entrepreneurs must make sure that their business skills are up to par. Even the most talented and hard-working arborists won't stand a chance if they can't balance their accounts or market their services properly.

Advancement to other industries related to arboriculture is another possibility. Some arborists choose to work in landscape design, forestry, or other fields of horticulture.

EARNINGS

The *Occupational Outlook Handbook* lists the 2003 median annual salary for arborists as $25,880 a year, with the bottom 10 percent earning $17,650 a year or less, and 10 percent earning $41,290 a year or more.

According to Derick Vanice, ISA's director of education programs, entry-level positions, such as grounds workers or trainees, can earn between $7 to $10 an hour; supervisors, with three or more years of experience, earn from $20 to $30 an hour; private consultants with eight to 10 years of experience, or arborists in sales positions, can earn $50,000 to $60,000 or more annually. Salaries vary greatly depending on many factors, among them the size of the company, the region, and the experience of the arborist. Arborists servicing busy urban areas tend to earn more.

Full-time employees receive a benefits package including health insurance, life insurance, paid vacation and sick time, and paid holidays. Most tree companies supply necessary uniforms, tools, equipment, and training.

WORK ENVIRONMENT

Much of an arborist's work is physically demanding, and most of it is done outdoors. Arborists work throughout the year, though their busiest time is in the spring and summer. Tasks done at this time include fertilizing, pruning, and prevention spraying. During the winter months, arborists can expect to care for trees injured or damaged by excess snow, ice storms, or floods.

Equipment such as sharp saws, grinders, chippers, bulldozers, tractors, and other large machinery can be potentially dangerous for arborists. There is also the risk of falling from the top of a tall tree, many of which reach heights of 50 feet or more. Arborists rely on cleated shoes, security belts, and safety hoists to make their job easier as well as safer.

OUTLOOK

The future of arboriculture has never looked so promising. The public's increasing interest in the planning and the preservation of the environment has increased demand for qualified arborists. Many homeowners are willing to pay top dollar for professionally designed and maintained landscaping. Research from Clemson University found that homes with professional landscaping sell for 6 to 7 percent higher than homes with lesser quality landscaping.

Increased resistance to pesticides and new species of insects pose constant threats to all trees. While travel abroad is easier and, in a sense, has made our world smaller, it has also placed our environment at risk. For example, Asian long-horn beetles were unknowingly transported to the United States via packing material. By the time the insects were discovered, the beetles had irreversibly damaged hundreds of mature trees throughout New York, Chicago, and surrounding areas. Arborists, especially those trained to diagnose and treat such cases, will be in demand to work in urban areas.

FOR MORE INFORMATION

For industry and career information, or to receive a copy of Arborist News *or* Careers in Arboriculture, *contact*
International Society of Arboriculture
PO 3129
Champaign, IL 61826-3129
Tel: 217-355-9411
Email: isa@isa-arbor.com
http://www.isa-arbor.com

For industry and career information, a listing of practicing arborists, or educational programs at the university level, or home study, contact
Tree Care Industry Association
3 Perimeter Road, Unit 1
Manchester, NH 03103
Tel: 800-733-2622
Email: TCIA@TreeCareIndustry.org
http://www.treecareindustry.org

For industry information, membership requirements, contact
Society of Municipal Arborists
PO Box 641
Watkinsville, GA 30677
Tel: 706-769-7412
Email: urbanforestry@prodigy.net
http://www.urban-forestry.com

Biochemists

QUICK FACTS

School Subjects
Biology
Chemistry

Personal Skills
Mechanical/manipulative
Technical/scientific

Work Environment
Primarily indoors
Primarily one location

Minimum Education Level
Bachelor's degree

Salary Range
$23,000 to $64,390 to
$110,030+

Certification or Licensing
Required in certain positions

Outlook
As fast as the average

DOT
041

GOE
02.03.03

NOC
2112

O*NET-SOC
19-1021.00, 19-1021.01

OVERVIEW

Biochemists explore the tiny world of the cell, study how illnesses develop, and search for ways to improve life on earth. Through studying the chemical makeup of living organisms, biochemists strive to understand the dynamics of life, from the secrets of cell-to-cell communication to the chemical changes in our brains that give us memories. Biochemists examine the chemical combinations and reactions involved in such functions as growth, metabolism, reproduction, and heredity. They also study the effect of environment on living tissue. If cancer is to be cured, the earth's pollution cleaned up, or the aging process slowed, it will be biochemists and molecular biologists who will help lead the way.

HISTORY

Biochemistry is a fairly new science, even though the concept of biochemistry is said to have its roots in the discovery of the fermentation process thousands of years ago. In fact, the basic steps used to make wine from grapes were the same in ancient times as they are today. However, the rather unchanging methods used for alcohol fermentation do not nearly reflect the revolutionary changes that have occurred throughout recent history in our knowledge of cell composition, growth, and function.

Robert Hooke, an English scientist, first described and named cells in 1665, when he looked at a slice of bark from an oak tree under a microscope with a magnifying power of 30x. Hooke never realized the significance of his discovery, however, because he thought the tiny boxes or "cells" he saw were unique to the bark. Anton van Leeuwenhoek, a Dutchman who lived in Hooke's time, discovered the existence of single-celled organisms by observing them in pond water and in animal blood and sperm. He used grains of sand that he had polished into magnifying glasses as powerful as 300x to see this invisible world. In 1839, nearly two centuries after Hooke's and Leeuwenhoek's discoveries, two German biologists, Matthias Schleiden and Theodor Schwann, correctly concluded that all living things consisted of cells. This theory was later expanded to include the idea that all cells come from other cells, and that the ability of cells to divide to form new cells is the basis for all reproduction, growth, and repair of many-celled organisms, like humans.

Over the past 40 years, a powerful instrument called the electron microscope has revealed the complex structure of cells. Every cell, at some state in its life, contains DNA, the genetic material that directs the cell's many activities. Biochemists have widened their scope to include the study of protein molecules and chromosomes, the building blocks of life itself. Biology and chemistry have always been allied sciences, and the exploration of cells and their molecular components, carried out by biochemists and other biological scientists, has revealed much about life. Watson and Crick's breakthrough discovery of the structure of DNA in 1953 touched off a flurry of scientific activity that led to a better and better understanding of DNA chemistry and the genetic code. These discoveries eventually made it possible to manipulate DNA, enabling genetic engineers to transplant foreign genes into microorganisms to produce such valuable products as human insulin, which occurred in 1982.

Today, the field of biochemistry crosses over into many other sciences, as biochemists have become involved in genetics, nutrition, psychology, fertility, agriculture, and more. The new biotechnology is revolutionizing the pharmaceutical industry. Much of this work is done by biochemists and molecular biologists because this technology involves understanding the complex chemistry of life.

THE JOB

Depending on a biochemist's education level and area of specialty, this professional can do many types of work for a variety of employers. For instance, a biochemist could have a job doing basic research for a federal government agency or for individual states with laboratories that employ skilled persons to analyze food, drug, air, water, waste, or animal tissue samples. A biochemist might work for a drug company as part of a basic research team searching for the cause of diseases or conduct applied research to develop drugs to cure disease. A biochemist might work in a biotechnology company focusing on the environment, energy, human health care, agriculture, or animal health. There, he or she might do research or quality control, or work on manufacturing/production or information systems. Another possibility is for the biochemist to specialize in an additional area, such as law, business, or journalism, and use his or her biochemistry or molecular biology background for a career that combines science with regulatory affairs, management, writing, or teaching.

Ph.D. scientists who enter the highest levels of academic life combine teaching and research. In addition to teaching in university classrooms and laboratories, they also do basic research designed to increase biochemistry and molecular biology knowledge. As Ph.D. scientists, these professionals could also work for an industry or government laboratory doing basic research or research and development (R&D). The problems studied, research styles, and type of organization vary widely across different laboratories. The Ph.D. scientist may lead a research group or be part of a small team of Ph.D. researchers. Other Ph.D. scientists might opt for administrative positions. In government, for example, these scientists might lead programs concerned with the safety of new devices, food, drugs, or pesticides and other chemicals. Or they might influence which projects will get federal funding.

Generally, biochemists employed in the United States work in one of three major fields: medicine, nutrition, or agriculture. In medicine, biochemists mass-produce life-saving chemicals usually found only in minuscule amounts in the body. Some of these chemicals have been helping diabetics and heart attack victims for years. Biochemists employed in the field of medicine might work to identify chemical changes in organs or cells that signal the development of such diseases as cancer, diabetes, or schizophrenia. Or they may look for chemical explanations for why certain people develop muscular dystrophy or become obese. While studying chemical makeup and changes in these situations, biochemists may work to discover a treatment or prevention for a disease. For instance, biochemists discovering how certain diseases such as AIDS and cancer escape detection by the immune system are also devising ways to enhance immunity to fight these diseases. Biochemists are also finding out the chemical basis of fertility and how to improve the success of in vitro fertilization to help couples have children or to preserve endangered species.

Biochemists in the pharmaceutical industry design, develop, and evaluate drugs, antibiotics, diagnostic kits, and other medical devices. They may search out ways to produce antibiotics, hormones, enzymes, or other drug components, or they may do quality control on the way in which drugs and dosages are made and determined.

In the field of nutrition, biochemists examine the effects of food on the body. For example, they might study the relationship between diet and diabetes. Biochemists doing this study could look at the nutrition content of certain foods eaten by people with diabetes and study how these foods affect the functioning of the pancreas and other organs. Biochemists in the nutrition field also look at vitamin and mineral deficiencies and how they affect the human body. They examine these deficiencies in relation to body performance, and they may study anything from how the liver is affected by a lack of vitamin B to the effects of poor nutrition on the ability to learn.

Biochemists involved in agriculture undertake studies to discover more efficient methods of crop cultivation, storage, and pest control. For example, they might create genetically engineered crops that are more resistant to frost, drought, spoilage, disease, and pests. They might focus on helping to create fruit trees that produce more fruit by studying the biochemical composition of the plant and determining how to alter or select for this desirable trait. Biochemists may study the chemical composition of insects to determine better and more efficient methods of controlling the pest population and the damage they do to crops. Or they could work on programming bacteria to clean up the environment by "eating" toxic chemicals.

About seven out of 10 biochemists are engaged in basic research, often for a university medical school or nonprofit organization, such as a foundation or research institute. The remaining 30 percent do applied research, using the discoveries of basic research to solve practical problems or develop products. For example, a biochemist working in basic research may make a discovery about how a living organism forms hormones. This discovery will lead to a scientist doing applied research, making hormones in the laboratory, and eventually to mass production. Discoveries made in DNA research have led to techniques for identifying criminals from a single strand of hair or a tiny blood stain left at the scene of a crime. The distinction between basic and applied research is one of degree, however; biochemists often engage in both types of work.

Biochemistry requires skillful use of a wide range of sophisticated analytical equipment and application of newly discovered techniques requiring special instruments or new chemical reagents. Sometimes, biochemists themselves must invent and test new instruments if existing methods and equipment do not meet their needs. Biochemists must also be patient, methodical, and careful in their laboratory procedures.

Biochemist Salaries

The following were the average annual salaries in 2003 for biochemists working in various industries:

Scientific research and development services	$68,300
Pharmaceutical and medicine manufacturing	$73,230
Colleges and universities	$49,030
Architectural and engineering services	$93,560
General medical and surgical hospitals	$72,030

Source: Bureau of Labor Statistics

REQUIREMENTS

Although they usually specialize in one of many areas in the field, biochemists and molecular biologists should also be familiar with several scientific disciplines, including chemistry, physics, mathematics, and computer science. High school can provide the foundation for getting this knowledge, while four years of college expands it, and postgraduate work directs students to explore specific areas more deeply. The following describes possible strategies at each level and includes a community college option.

High School

If you have an interest in biochemistry as a high school student, you should take at least one year each of biology, chemistry, physics, algebra, geometry, and trigonometry. Introductory calculus is also a good idea. Because scientists must clearly and accurately communicate their results verbally and in writing, English courses that emphasize writing skills are strongly recommended. Many colleges and universities also require several years of a foreign language, a useful skill in this day and age, as scientists frequently exchange information with researchers from other countries.

Postsecondary Training

Some colleges have their own special requirements for admission, so you should do a little research and take any special courses you need for the college that interests you. Also, check the catalogs of colleges and universities to see if they offer a program in biochemistry or related sciences. Some schools award a bachelor's degree in biochemistry, and nearly all colleges and universities offer a major in biology or chemistry.

To best prepare yourself for a career in biochemistry or molecular biology, you should start by earning a bachelor's degree in either of these two areas. Even if your college does not offer a specific program in biochemistry or molecular biology, you can get comparable training by doing one of two things: (1) working toward a bachelor's degree in chemistry and taking courses in biology, molecular genetics, and biochemistry, including a biochemistry laboratory class, or (2) earning a bachelor's degree in biology, but taking more chemistry, mathematics, and physics courses than the biology major may require, and also choosing a biochemistry course that has lab work with it.

It really doesn't matter if you earn a bachelor of science (B.S.) or a bachelor of arts (B.A.) degree; some schools offer both. It is more important to choose your courses thoughtfully and to get advice in your freshman year from a faculty member who knows about the fields of biochemistry and molecular biology.

Many careers in biochemistry, especially those that involve teaching at a college or directing scientific research at a university, a government laboratory, or a commercial company, require at least a master's degree and prefer a doctorate or Ph.D. degree. Most students enter graduate programs with a bachelor's degree in biochemistry, or in chemistry or biology with supplementary courses. Because biochemistry and molecular biology are so broad-based, you can enter their graduate programs from such diverse fields as physics, psychology, nutrition, microbiology, or engineering. Graduate schools prefer students with laboratory or research experience.

However you get there, a graduate education program is intense. A master's degree requires about a year of course work and often a research project as well. For a Ph.D. degree, full-time course work can last up to two years, followed by one or more special test exams. But the most important part of Ph.D. training is the requirement for all students to conduct an extensive research project leading to significant new scientific findings. Most students work under a faculty member's direction. This training is vital, as it will help you develop the skills to frame scientific questions and discover ways to answer them. It will also teach you important laboratory skills useful in tackling other biochemical problems. Most students complete a Ph.D. program in four or five years.

Certification or Licensing

Biochemists who wish to work in a hospital may need certification by a national certifying board such as the American Board of Clinical Chemistry.

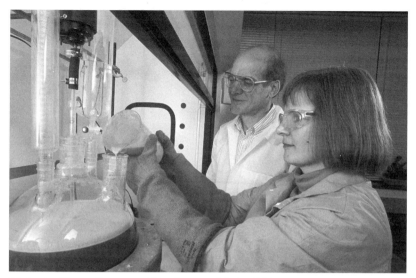

Biologist Karen Scott and biochemist Michael Haas prepare a reactor of soybean-derived soapstock for conversion to biodiesel. *(Photo by Peggy Greb/USDA)*

Other Requirements

A scientist never stops learning, even when formal education has ended. This is particularly true for biochemists and molecular biologists because constant breakthroughs and technology advances make for a constantly changing work environment. That is why most Ph.D.s go for more research experience (postdoctoral research) before they enter the workplace. As a "postdoc," you would not take course work, earn a degree, or teach; you would be likely to work full-time on a high-level research project in the laboratory of an established scientist. Typically, this postdoctoral period lasts two to three years, during which time you would get a salary or be supported by a fellowship. Though not essential for many industry research jobs, postdoctoral research is generally expected of those wishing to become professors. Also, because biochemistry and medicine are such allies, some Ph.D. recipients also earn a doctor of medicine degree (M.D.) as a physician does. This is to get the broadest possible base for a career in medical research.

EXPLORING

The analytical, specialized nature of most biochemistry makes it unlikely that you will gain much exposure to it before college. Many high school chemistry and biology courses, however, allow students to work with laboratory tools and techniques that will give them a valuable background before college. In some cases, high school students can take advantage of opportunities to train as laboratory technicians by taking courses at a community college. You might also want to contact local colleges, universities, or laboratories to set up interviews with biochemists to learn as much as you can about the field. In addition, reading science and medical magazines will help you to stay current with recent breakthroughs in the biochemistry field.

EMPLOYERS

Government agencies at the federal, state, and local levels employ about four out of every 10 biological scientists. At such agencies these scientists may do basic research and analyze food, drug, air, water, waste, or animal tissue samples. Biochemists also work for university medical schools or nonprofit organizations, such as a foundation or research institute, doing basic research. Drug companies employ biochemists to search for the causes of diseases or develop drugs to cure them. Biochemists work in quality control, research, manufacturing/production, or information systems at biotechnology companies that concentrate on the environment, energy, human health care, agriculture, or animal health. Universities hire biochemists to teach in combination with doing research.

STARTING OUT

A bachelor's degree in biochemistry or molecular biology can help you get into medical, dental, veterinary, law, or business school. It can also be a stepping-stone to a career in many different but related fields: biotechnology, toxicology, biomedical engineering, clinical chemistry, plant pathology, animal science, or other fields. Biochemists fresh from a college undergraduate program can take advantage of opportunities to get valuable on-the-job experience in a biochemistry or molecular biology laboratory. The National Science Foundation and the National Institutes of Health, both federal government agencies, sponsor research programs for undergraduates. Groups who can particularly benefit from these programs include women, Hispanics, African Americans, Native Americans, Native Alaskans, and students with disabilities. Your college or university may also offer senior research projects that provide hands-on experience.

Another way to improve your chances of getting a job is to spend an additional year at a university with training programs for specialized laboratory techniques. Researchers and companies like these "certificate programs" because they teach valuable skills related to cell culture, genetic engineering, recombinant DNA technology, biotechnology, in vitro cell biology, protein engineering, or DNA sequencing and synthesis. In some universities, you can work toward a bachelor's degree and a certificate at the same time.

Biochemists with a bachelor's degree usually begin work in industry or government as research assistants doing testing and analysis. In the drug industry, for example, you might analyze the ingredients of a product to verify and maintain its quality. Biochemists with a master's degree may enter the field in management, marketing, or sales positions, whereas those with a doctorate usually go into basic or applied research. Many Ph.D. graduates work at colleges and universities where the emphasis is on teaching.

ADVANCEMENT

The more education you have, the greater your reward potential. Biochemists with a graduate degree have more opportunities for advancement than those with only an undergraduate degree. It is not uncommon for students to go back to graduate school after working for a while in a job that required a lesser degree. Some graduate students become research or teaching assistants in colleges and universities, qualifying for professorships when they receive their advanced degrees. Having a doctorate allows you to design research initiatives and direct others in carrying out experiments. Experienced biochemists with doctorates can move up to high-level administrative positions and supervise entire research programs. Other highly qualified biochemists who prefer to devote themselves to research often become leaders in a particular aspect of their profession.

EARNINGS

According to a report by the National Association of Colleges and Employers, beginning salaries in 2003 for graduates with bachelor's degrees in biological science ranged from $23,000 to $35,000.

The following mid-range earnings for R&D biochemists came from a report by Abbott, Langer and Associates: $52,000 for managers, $58,064 for R&D specialists, $83,500 for directors, and $90,479 for section heads. A report from the American Chemical Society gives the following industry earnings: $47,251 for biochemists with a bachelor's degree, $56,205 for those with a master's degree, and $79,176 for doctoral degree holders.

The U.S. Department of Labor reports that biochemists and biophysicists had average annual incomes of $64,390 in 2003. Salaries ranged from less than $37,460 to more than $110,030.

Colleges and universities also employ many biochemists as professors and researchers. The American Association of University Professors reports that salaries for postsecondary teachers with Ph.D.'s range from $45,763 for a lecturer to $100,682 for a full tenured professor.

Biochemists who work for universities, the government, or industry all tend to receive good benefits packages, such as health and life insurance, pension plans, and paid vacation and sick leave. Those employed as university faculty operate on the academic calendar, which means that they can get summer and winter breaks from teaching classes.

WORK ENVIRONMENT

Biochemists generally work in clean, quiet, and well-lighted laboratories where physical labor is minimal. They must, however, take the proper precautions in handling chemicals and organic substances that could be dangerous or cause illness. They may work with plants and animals; their tissues, cells, and products; and with yeast and bacteria.

Biochemists in industry generally work a 40-hour week, although they, like their counterparts in research, often put in many extra hours. They must be ready to spend a considerable amount of time keeping up with current literature, for example. Many biochemists occasionally travel to attend meetings or conferences. Those in research write papers for presentation at meetings or for publication in scientific journals.

Individuals interested in biochemistry must have the patience to work for long periods of time on a project without necessarily getting the desired results. Biochemistry is often a team affair, requiring an ability to work well and cooperate with others. Successful biochemists are continually learning and increasing their skills.

OUTLOOK

Employment growth for biological scientists, including biochemists, is expected to be about as fast as the average through 2012, according to the U.S. Department of Labor, as the number of trained scientists has increased faster than available funding. Competition will be strong for basic research positions, and candidates with more education and the experience it brings will be more likely to find the positions they want. Employment is available in health-related fields, where the emphasis is on finding cures for such diseases as cancer, muscular dystrophy, AIDS, and Alzheimer's. Additional jobs will be created to produce genetically engineered drugs and other products in the new and rapidly expanding field of genetic engineering. In this area, the outlook is best for biochemists with advanced degrees who can conduct genetic and cellular research. A caveat exists, however. Employment growth may slow somewhat as the number of new biotechnology firms slows and existing firms merge. Biochemists with bachelor's degrees who have difficulty entering their chosen career field may find openings as technicians or technologists or may choose to transfer their skills to other biological science fields.

It is estimated that over the next decade, 68 percent of those entering the workforce will be women and members of other minority groups. The federal government, recognizing this situation, offers a variety of special programs (through the National Science Foundation and the National Institutes of Health) to bring women, minorities, and persons with disabilities into the field.

FOR MORE INFORMATION

For additional information about careers, education, and scholarships, contact the following organizations:

American Association for Clinical Chemistry
2101 L Street, NW, Suite 202
Washington, DC 20037-1558
Tel: 800-892-1400
Email: info@aacc.org
http://www.aacc.org

American Chemical Society
1155 16th Street, NW
Washington, DC 20036
Tel: 800-227-5558
http://www.chemistry.org

American Institute of Biological Sciences
1444 Eye Street, NW, Suite 200
Washington, DC 20005
Tel: 202-628-1500
Email: admin@aibs.org
http://www.aibs.org

American Society for Biochemistry and Molecular Biology
Education Information
9650 Rockville Pike
Bethesda, MD 20814-3996
Tel: 301-530-7145
Email: asbmb@asbmb.faseb.org
http://www.asbmb.org

American Society for Investigative Pathology
9650 Rockville Pike
Bethesda, MD 20814-3993
Tel: 301-530-7130
Email: asip@asip.org
http://www.asip.org

Biologists

QUICK FACTS

School Subjects
Biology
Physiology

Personal Skills
Mechanical/manipulative
Technical/scientific

Work Environment
Indoors and outdoors
Primarily multiple locations

Minimum Education Level
Bachelor's degree

Salary Range
$33,930 to $60,390 to
$102,930

Certification or Licensing
Required for certain
positions

Outlook
About as fast as the average

DOT
041

GOE
02.03.01, 02.03.03

NOC
2121

O*NET-SOC
19-1020.01, 19-1021.00,
19-1022.00, 19-1023.00

OVERVIEW

Biologists study the origin, development, anatomy, function, distribution, and other basic principles of living organisms. They are concerned with the nature of life itself in humans, microorganisms, plants, and animals, and with the relationship of each organism to its environment. Biologists perform research in many specialties that advance the fields of medicine, agriculture, and industry. Approximately 75,000 biological scientists are employed in the United States.

HISTORY

The biological sciences developed slowly over the course of human history. Early humans practiced an inexact form of biology when they established agriculture. They observed the environment around them to determine what types of seeds yielded consumable food, when to plant, when to water, and when to harvest the seeds for planting in the next season. Early humans improved their way of life as a result of their primitive forays into science.

It wasn't until modern times that biology developed into an exact science. Our ancestors learned to differentiate between desirable and undesirable plants (taxonomy), to seek out and live in more habitable environments (ecology), to domesticate plants (agronomy and horticulture) and animals (animal husbandry), and to eat a suitable diet (nutrition). Eventually, plants and animals were classified; later they were studied to see how they functioned and how they related to other organisms around them. This was the beginning of zoology (animal science) and botany (plant science).

The Greek philosopher Aristotle created one of the first documented taxonomic systems for animals. He divided animals into two types: blooded (mammals, birds, amphibians, reptiles, and fishes) and bloodless (insects, crustaceans, and other lower animals). He also studied reproduction and theorized, incorrectly, how embryos developed in animals.

From the second century to the 11th century, the Arabs made important advances in biological understanding. Unlike the Europeans, they continued to study from the base of knowledge established by the Greeks. Avicenna, a Persian philosopher and physician, wrote the *Canon of Medicine,* one of the most influential and important publications on medical knowledge in the world at its time—and for the next seven centuries.

The field of biology has expanded rapidly in the last two centuries. The French physician Louis Pasteur developed the field of immunology, and his studies of fermentation led to modern microbiology. Many other achievements became possible because of improvements in the microscope. Scientists could isolate much smaller structures than ever before possible. Matthias Schleiden and Theodor Schwann formulated the idea that the cell is the fundamental unit of all organisms. Gregor Mendel discovered the principles of heredity through crossbreeding pea plants.

While the 19th century can be considered the age of cellular biology, the 20th and early 21st centuries have been dominated by studies and breakthroughs in biochemistry and molecular biology. The discovery of the atomic structure allowed the fundamental building blocks of nature to be studied. Living tissues were found to be composed of fats, sugars, and proteins. Proteins were found to be composed of amino acids. Discoveries in cell biology established the manner in which information was transmitted from one organism to its progeny. Chromosomes were recognized as the carriers of this information. In 1944, Oswald Avery and a team of scientists were able to isolate and identify DNA as the transmitter of genetic information. In 1953 James Watson and Francis Crick deciphered the complex structure of DNA and hypothesized that it carried the genetic code for all living matter.

Biological science is the foundation for most of the discoveries that affect people's everyday lives. Biologists break new ground to improve our health and quality of life and help us to better understand the world around us.

THE JOB

Biology can be divided into many specialties. The biologist, who studies a wide variety of living organisms, has interests that differ from those of the chemist, physicist, and geologist, who are concerned with nonliving matter. Biologists, or *life scientists*, may be identified by their specialties. Following is a breakdown of the many kinds of biologists and their specific fields of study:

Anatomists study animal bodies from basic cell structure to complex tissues and organs. They determine the ability of body parts to regenerate and investigate the possibility of transplanting organs and skin. Their research is applied to human medicine.

Aquatic biologists study animals and plants that live in water and how they are affected by their environmental conditions, such as the salt, acid, and oxygen content of the water and temperature, light, and other factors.

Biochemists study the chemical composition of living organisms. They attempt to understand the complex reactions involved in reproduction, growth, metabolism, and heredity.

Biophysicists apply physical principles to biological problems. They study the mechanics, heat, light, radiation, sound, electricity, and energetics of living cells and organisms and do research in the areas of vision, hearing, brain function, nerve conduction, muscle reflex, and damaged cells and tissues.

Bio-technicians, or *biological technicians*, assist the cornucopia of biological scientists in their endeavors.

Botanists study plant life. Some specialize in plant biochemistry, the structure and function of plant parts, and identification and classification, among other topics.

Cytologists, sometimes called *cell biologists*, examine the cells of plants and animals, including those cells involved in reproduction. They use microscopes and other instruments to observe the growth and division of cells and to study the influences of physical and chemical factors on both normal and malignant cells.

Ecologists examine such factors as pollutants, rainfall, altitude, temperature, and population size in order to study the distribution and abundance of organisms and their relation to their environment.

Entomologists study insects and their relationship to other life forms.

Geneticists study heredity in various forms of life. They are concerned with how biological traits such as color, size, and resistance to disease originate and are transmitted from one generation to another. They also try to develop ways to alter or produce new traits, using chemicals, heat, light, or other means.

Histopathologists investigate diseased tissue in humans and animals.

Immunologists study the manner in which the human body resists disease.

Limnologists study freshwater organisms and their environment.

Marine biologists specialize in the study of marine species and their environment. They gather specimens at different times, taking into account tidal cycles, seasons, and exposure to atmospheric elements, in order to answer questions concerning the overall health of sea organisms and their environment.

Microbiologists study bacteria, viruses, molds, algae, yeasts, and other organisms of microscopic or submicroscopic size. Some microorganisms are useful to humans; they are studied and used in the production of food, such as cheese, bread, and tofu. Other microorganisms have been used to preserve food and tenderize meat. Some microbiologists work with microorganisms that cause disease. They work to diagnose, treat, and prevent disease. Microbiologists have helped prevent typhoid fever, influenza, measles, polio, whooping cough, and smallpox. Today, they work on cures for AIDS, cancer, cystic fibrosis, and Alzheimer's disease, among others.

Molecular biologists apply their research on animal and bacterial systems toward the goal of improving and better understanding human health.

Mycologists study edible, poisonous, and parasitic fungi, such as mushrooms, molds, yeasts, and mildews, to determine which are useful to medicine, agriculture, and industry. Their research has resulted in benefits such as the development of antibiotics, the propagation of mushrooms, and methods of retarding fabric deterioration.

Nematologists study nematodes (roundworms), which are parasitic in animals and plants. Nematodes transmit diseases, attack insects, or attack other nematodes that exist in soil or water. Nematologists investigate and develop methods of controlling these organisms.

Parasitologists study animal parasites and their effects on humans and other animals.

Pharmacologists may be employed as researchers by pharmaceutical companies. They often spend most of their time working in the laboratory, where they study the effects of various drugs and medical compounds on mice or rabbits. Working within controlled environments, pharmacologists precisely note the types, quantities, and timing of medicines administered as a part of their experiments. Periodically, they make blood smears or perform autopsies to study different reactions. They usually work with a team of researchers, headed by one with a doctorate and consisting of several biologists with master's and bachelor's degrees and some laboratory technicians.

Physiologists are biologists who specialize in studying all the life stages of plants or animals. Some specialize in a particular body system or a particular function, such as respiration.

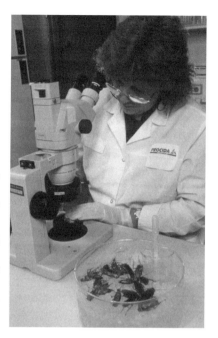

This Biologist is placing a cockroach (order *Blattodea*) under a microscope. Other cockroaches are being kept fresh in the ice-filled container at bottom center until they are studied. Some species of cockroach are household pests. *(Pascal Goetgheluck/ Photo Researchers Inc.)*

Wildlife biologists study the habitats and the conditions necessary for the survival of birds and other wildlife. Their goal is to find ways to ensure the continuation of healthy wildlife populations, while lessening the impact and growth of civilization around them.

Zoologists study all types of animals to learn their origin, interrelationships, classifications, life histories, habits, diseases, relation to the environment, growth, genetics, and distribution. Zoologists are usually identified by the animals they study: *ichthyologists* (fish), *mammalogists* (mammals), *ornithologists* (birds), and *herpetologists* (reptiles and amphibians).

Biologists may also work for government agencies concerned with public health. *Toxicologists*, for example, study the effects of toxic substances on humans, animals, and plants. The data they gather are used in consumer protection and industrial safety programs to reduce the hazards of accidental exposure or ingestion. *Public-health microbiologists* conduct experiments on water, foods, and the general environment of a community to detect the presence of harmful bacteria so pollution and contagious diseases can be controlled or eliminated.

REQUIREMENTS

High School

High school students interested in a career in biology should take English, biology, physics, chemistry, Latin, geometry, and algebra.

Postsecondary Training

Prospective biologists should also obtain broad undergraduate college training. In addition to courses in all phases of biology, useful related courses include organic and inorganic chemistry, physics, and mathematics. Modern languages, English, biometrics (the use of mathematics in biological measurements), and statistics are also useful. Courses in computers will be extremely beneficial. Students should take advantage of courses that require laboratory, field, or collecting work.

Nearly all institutions offer undergraduate training in one or more of the biological sciences. These vary from liberal arts schools that offer basic majors in botany and zoology to large universities that permit specialization in areas such as entomology, bacteriology, and physiology at the undergraduate level.

The best way to become a biologist is to earn a bachelor's degree in biology or one of its specialized fields, such as anatomy, bacteriology, botany, ecology, or microbiology. For the highest professional status, a doctorate is required. This is particularly true of top research positions and most higher-level college teaching openings. Many colleges and universities offer courses leading to a master's degree and a doctorate. A study made by the National Science Foundation showed that among a group of biologists listed on the National Scientific Manpower Register, 10 percent held a bachelor's degree, 33 percent held a master's or professional medical degree, and the remaining 57 percent had earned a doctorate.

Candidates for a doctorate specialize in one of the subdivisions of biology. A number of sources of financial assistance are available to finance graduate work. Most major universities have a highly developed fellowship (scholarship) or assistantship (part-time teaching or research) program.

Organizations, such as the U.S. Public Health Service and the National Science Foundation, make awards to support graduate students. In a recent year, for example, the Public Health Service made 8,000 fellowship and training grants. In addition, major universities often hold research contracts or have their own projects that provide part-time and summer employment for undergraduate and graduate students.

Certification or Licensing

A state license may be required for biologists who are employed as technicians in general service health organizations, such as hospitals or clinics. To qualify for this license, proof of suitable educational background is necessary.

Other Requirements

Biologists must be systematic in their approach to solving the problems that they face. They should have probing, inquisitive minds and an aptitude for biology, chemistry, and mathematics. Patience and imagination are also required since they may spend much time in observation and analysis. Biologists must also have good communication skills in order to effectively gather and exchange data and solve problems that arise in their work.

EXPLORING

Students can measure their aptitude and interest in the work of the biologist by taking courses in the field. Laboratory assignments, for example, provide information on techniques used by the working biologist. Many schools hire students as laboratory assistants to work directly under a teacher and help administer the laboratory sections of courses.

School assemblies, field trips to federal and private laboratories and research centers, and career conferences provide additional insight into career opportunities. Advanced students often are able to attend professional meetings and seminars.

Part-time and summer positions in biology or related areas are particularly helpful. Students with some college courses in biology may find summer positions as laboratory assistants. Graduate students may find work on research projects conducted by their institutions. Beginning college and advanced high school students may find employment as laboratory aides or hospital orderlies or attendants. Despite the menial nature of these positions, they afford a useful insight into careers in biology. High school students often have the opportunity to join volunteer service groups at local hospitals. Student science training programs (SSTPs) allow qualified high school students to spend a summer doing research under the supervision of a scientist.

EMPLOYERS

Approximately half of all biological scientists work for the government at the federal, state, or local level. The majority of those who do not work for the government are involved in the drug industry, which includes pharmaceutical companies, hospitals, biotechnology companies, and laboratories. The area in which biologists work is influenced by their specialties. Marine biologists, for example, can find employment with the U.S. Department of Interior, the U.S. Fish

Profile: Carolus Linnaeus (1707–1778)

Swedish naturalist Linnaeus developed systematic methods for classifying and naming plants and animals. He devised the classifications of class, order, genus, and species, and established as standard the binomial (two-name) system for giving scientific names to plants and animals. Linnaeus placed human beings in the order of primates, giving our species the scientific name *Homo sapiens*. Linnaeus classified thousands of plant species, assigning plants to 24 classes according to the number and position of their stamens and pistils. Although later botanical knowledge revealed that this system was inadequate, it did lay the foundation for the science of plant taxonomy, as well as for Darwin's theory of evolution.

Here, for instance, is the classification of the domestic dog, *Canis familiaris*:
Kingdom: Animalia (animals)
Phylum: Chordata (animals with a spinal cord)
Subphylum: Vertebrata (vertebrate)
Class: Mammalia (mammals)
Subclass: Theria (mammals that give birth to live young)
Order: Carnivora (carnivores)
Family: Canidae (related animals, such as coyotes, dogs, foxes, jackals, and wolves, some of which can cross-breed)
Genus: Canis (dog)
Species: familiaris (domesticated dog)

Classification of the cork oak tree, *Quercus suber*:
Kingdom: Plantae (plants)
Subkingdom: Tracheophyta (plants with a vascular system)
Division: Anthophyta (flowering plants)
Class: Dicotyledonae (seed plants that produce embryos with paired cotyledons and net-veined leaves)
Order: Fagales (a collection of similar families of trees)
Family: Fagaceae (beeches and other trees, chiefly having unisexual flowers)
Genus: Quercus (Latin for the oak tree)
Species: suber (Latin for "to be in season")

and Wildlife Service, and the National Oceanic and Atmospheric Administration. They may also find employment in nongovernmental agencies, such as the Scripps Institution of Oceanography in California and the Marine Biological Laboratory in Massachusetts. Microbiologists can find employment with the U.S. Department of

Health and Human Services, the Environmental Protection Agency, and the Department of Agriculture, among others. They may also work for pharmaceutical, food, agricultural, geological, environmental, and pollution control companies. Wildlife biologists can find employment with the U.S. Public Health Service, the U.S. Fish and Wildlife Service, and the Forest Service, among many others.

STARTING OUT

Biologists who are interested in becoming teachers should consult their college placement offices. Public and private high schools and an increasing number of colleges hire teachers through the colleges at which they studied. Private employment agencies also place a significant number of teachers. Some teaching positions are filled through direct application.

Biologists interested in private industry and nonprofit organizations may also apply directly for employment. Major organizations that employ biologists often interview college seniors on campus. Private and public employment offices frequently have listings from these employers. Experienced biologists often change positions as a result of contacts made at professional seminars and national conventions.

Special application procedures are required for positions with government agencies. Civil service applications for federal, state, and municipal positions may be obtained by writing to the agency involved and from high school and college guidance and placement bureaus, public employment agencies, and post offices.

ADVANCEMENT

In a field as broad as biology, numerous opportunities for advancement exist. To a great extent, however, advancement depends on the individual's level of education. A doctorate is generally required for college teaching, independent research, and top-level administrative and management jobs. A master's degree is sufficient for some jobs in applied research, and a bachelor's degree may qualify for some entry-level jobs.

With the right qualifications, the biologist may advance to the position of project chief and direct a team of other biologists. Many use their knowledge and experience as background for administrative and management positions. Often, as they develop professional expertise, biologists move from strictly technical assignments into positions in which they interpret biological knowledge.

The usual path of advancement in biology, as in other sciences, comes from specialization and the development of the status of an expert in a given field. Biologists may work with professionals in other major fields to explore problems that require an interdisciplinary approach, such as biochemistry, biophysics, biostatistics (or biometrics). Biochemistry, for example, uses the methods of chemistry to study the composition of biological materials and the molecular mechanisms of biological processes.

EARNINGS

Earnings for biological scientists vary extensively based on the type and size of their employer, the individual's level of education and experience, and the area of biology in which the scientist specializes. The median salary for all biological scientists was $60,390 in 2002, as reported by the U.S. Department of Labor. In 2003 general biological scientists working for the federal government earned an average annual salary of $66,262. Those specializing in certain areas tended to have slightly higher annual incomes. Ecologists, for example, had an average salary of $65,207 per year; microbiologists reported an average of $73,513; geneticists averaged $78,652; and physiologists, $85,181.

According to the National Association of Colleges and Employers, those with bachelor's degrees in the biological sciences had beginning salaries averaging $23,000–$35,000 per year in 2003. In general, the highest salaries were earned by biologists in business and industry, followed by those self-employed, working for nonprofit organizations, in military service, and working for the U.S. Public Health Service or other positions in the federal government. The lowest salaries were earned by teachers and by those working for various state and local governments.

Biologists are usually eligible for health and dental insurance, paid vacations and sick days, and retirement plans. Some employers may offer reimbursement for continuing education, seminars, and travel.

WORK ENVIRONMENT

The biologist's work environment varies greatly depending upon the position and type of employer. One biologist may work outdoors or travel much of the time. Another wears a white smock and spends years working in a laboratory. Some work with toxic substances and disease cultures; strict safety measures must be observed.

Biologists frequently work under pressure. For example, those employed by pharmaceutical houses work in an atmosphere of keen competition for sales that encourages the development of new drug products, and, as they are identified, the rapid testing and early marketing of these products. The work is very exacting, however, and pharmaceutical biologists must exercise great care to ensure that adequate testing of products has been properly conducted.

Some biologists, including botanists, ecologists, and zoologists, may undertake strenuous, sometimes dangerous, fieldwork in primitive conditions. Marine biologists work in the field, on research ships or in laboratories, in tropical seas and ocean areas with considerably cooler climates. They will be required to perform some strenuous work, such as carrying a net, digging, chipping, or hauling equipment or specimens. Marine biologists who work underwater must be able to avoid hazards, such as razor-sharp coral reefs and other underwater dangers. Wildlife biologists work in all types of weather and in all types of terrain and ecosystems. They may work alone or with a group in inhospitable surroundings in order to gather information.

OUTLOOK

The U.S. Department of Labor predicts employment for biological scientists to be as fast as average through 2012, although competition will be stiff for some positions. For example, Ph.D.'s looking for research positions will find strong competition for a limited number of openings. Government funding is currently plentiful (some 1 in 3 applications for research grants are approved), but a recession or shift in political power can cause the loss of funding for grants and the decline of research and development endeavors.

Private industry will need biologists to work in sales, marketing, and research management. Companies developing new drugs, modified crops, environmentally friendly products, and the like will need the expertise of biological scientists. The U.S. Department of Labor also predicts that even companies not solely involved in biotechnology will be increasingly using biotechnology developments and techniques in their businesses. This should cause more job opportunities for biological scientists in a variety of industries.

Biologists with advanced degrees will be best qualified for the most lucrative and challenging jobs, although this varies by specialty, with genetic, cellular, and biochemical research showing the most promise. Scientists with bachelor's degrees may find openings as science or engineering technicians or as health technologists and technicians. Many colleges and universities are cutting back on their faculties, but high schools and two-year colleges may have teaching positions available.

FOR MORE INFORMATION

For information on careers in biology, contact
  American Institute of Biological Sciences
  1444 Eye Street, NW, Suite 200
  Washington, DC 20005
  Tel: 202-628-1500
  Email: admin@aibs.org
  http://www.aibs.org

For a career brochure, career-related articles, and a list of institutions that award academic degrees with a major in physiology, contact
  American Physiological Society
  9650 Rockville Pike
  Bethesda, MD 20814-3991
  Tel: 301-634-7164
  http://www.the-aps.org

For information on careers, educational resources, and fellowships, contact
  American Society for Microbiology
  1752 N Street, NW
  Washington, DC 20036
  Tel: 202-737-3600
  http://www.asm.org

For career information, including articles and books, contact
  Biotechnology Industry Organization
  1225 Eye Street, NW, Suite 400
  Washington, DC 20005
  Tel: 202-962-9200
  http://www.bio.org

For information on careers in the marine sciences, contact
  National Aquarium in Baltimore
  501 East Pratt Street, Pier 3
  Baltimore, MD 21202-3194
  Tel: 410-576-3800
  http://www.aqua.org

For information on specific careers in biology, contact
National Institutes of Health
9000 Rockville Pike
Bethesda, MD 20892
Tel: 301-435-1908
Email: orsinfo@mail.nih.gov
http://www.nih.gov

For information on specific careers, contact the FDA's job hotline.
U.S. Food and Drug Administration (FDA)
5600 Fishers Lane
Rockville, MD 20857-0001
Tel: 888-463-6332
http://www.fda.gov

―――――――― **INTERVIEW** ――――――――

Joseph Panno holds a Ph.D. in biology from Simon Fraser University (SFU), British Columbia. He has conducted extensive research in the fields of molecular biology and physiology and has taught a variety of undergraduate biology courses. A full-time writer, he is the co-author of Insect Aging, *a book describing cellular changes with age in a variety of insect species, and he has recently completed a six-volume set of science books titled* The New Biology, *which deals with all facets of current research in the field of biology, including stem cell therapy, animal cloning, and gene therapy. Dr. Panno shared his insights and experiences with the editors of* Careers in Focus: Biology.

Q. What led you to pursue a career in biology?

A. I have always been interested in things biological. As a child of 9 or 10 I kept a small menagerie in my backyard that consisted of pigeons, chickens, ducks, turtles, and the occasional mangy dog. But at that time, I never dreamed I would become a biologist. Indeed, during the 1970s, when I was in my 20s, I made my living as a sculptor and was happy doing so, but I had the feeling that if I knew more about biology it might help my artwork. So, I took a few courses in the subject and eventually found myself close to graduation. Through it all, I had planned to stick with my career as a starving artist, but in my last year I took an undergraduate research course from the late Dr. Karun Nair at SFU. At the time, Dr. Nair had one of only three computerized cell image analyzers in all of North America, and my job was to analyze the DNA content in various insects in order to refine their taxonomic relationships. I found the application of computer technology to biological research completely fascinating and, well, I was hooked. Immediately after graduating, Dr. Nair hired me as his research assistant and we began to study the way cell nuclei change in aging houseflies—a research project that quickly turned into my master's thesis. From there, the Ph.D. was inevitable.

Q. How did your academic experiences help prepare you for your career?

A. Of course, the undergraduate science curriculum gives the student the basics to succeed as a biologist. But it was the research course I took that put me on the road to a career in biology. That course, simply by showing me firsthand how exciting research can be, was all I needed.

I began my research career in 1980 when I entered the master's program in the Department of Biology at SFU. My thesis dealt with the cell biology of aging and computer-assisted analysis of cell structure and function. I received a master's degree in 1984 and was made a research associate in a histochemistry laboratory at SFU. In collaboration with a cytogenetics laboratory at Vancouver General Hospital, I helped develop a computerized diagnostic system for the detection of Down's syndrome and other cytogenetic diseases. This involved writing computer software and developing some of the procedures for processing the tissue samples. It was during this period that my interests began to shift from gerontology (the study of the aging process) to cancer research, as several laboratories in North America began using computerized image analyzers for cancer diagnosis.

In 1990, I entered the Ph.D. program at SFU and conducted my research in a laboratory specializing in vertebrate endocrinology (the study of hormone-producing tissues). This work involved the cloning and characterization of the *myc* proto-oncogene from the pituitary gland (master endocrine gland) of the rainbow trout. The *myc* gene, when behaving abnormally, is one of the most potent cancer-causing agents in the human population. My research described the normal physiological function of this gene based on its expression profile *in vivo* and in cultured pituitary glands.

While in graduate school I taught or tutored a variety of university biology courses. After receiving my Ph.D. in 1996, I taught a course in animal physiology before turning to a career as a writer.

Q. What is your main focus at this point in your career?

A. These days, my time is devoted entirely to writing, an occupation that I enjoy as much as research or teaching. I am currently working on a history of the biological and medical sciences titled *Science for Sorcerers*.

Q. What do you see as the pros and cons of a career in biology?

A. Research in biology has never been more exciting than it is right now. The topics that I wrote about in *The New Biology*, such as stem cell research and animal cloning, are about to revolution-ize our understanding of the cell and our ability to treat a host of terrible diseases and physical injuries. Because of these new technologies, the number of job opportunities has increased dramatically in academia as well as in the pharmaceutical and biotechnology sectors.

On the down side, a career in biology can be very demanding in terms of the number of hours research biologists often work each week. This can make it difficult for young scientists to start a family and to spend time with their children. This problem is especially pronounced for highly competitive areas, such as stem cell research. Recently, a research team in South Korea described an improved method for obtaining embryonic stem cells. These scientists worked virtually nonstop—no holidays and no week-ends off—for over two years to obtain these results.

Q. What would you say are the most important skills and per-sonal qualities for someone interested in pursuing a career in biology?

A. Being bright helps, but the issue is more complex than that. Very bright people often fail in this business because they lack the determination and focus that a researcher needs in order to see a project through to the end. In some cases, students are simply afraid to tackle a project because it looks difficult. Research is not for the faint of heart. Students who are successful love a chal-lenge, refuse to give up, enjoy discussing their work with others and, by design or good luck, manage to find supervisors who act like true mentors.

Q. What advice do you have for someone who is interested in entering this field?

A. Study hard as an undergraduate and try not to go crazy. By that I mean, work hard but have some fun as well and don't sink into a deep depression if you get less than an A in some of your courses. Also, try to decide by the end of your second year the direction you're going to take, whether it's medical school, graduate school, botany, molecular biology, and so forth. This will help you focus during your final two years and, should you decide to go into research, will greatly simplify your search for an appropriate graduate school.

Biomedical Engineers

QUICK FACTS

School Subjects
Biology
Chemistry

Personal Skills
Helping/teaching
Technical/scientific

Work Environment
Primarily indoors
Primarily one location

Minimum Education Level
Bachelor's degree

Salary Range
$38,250 to $60,410 to
$94,270

Certification or Licensing
Voluntary

Outlook
Faster than the average

DOT
019

GOE
02.07.04

NOC
2148

O*NET-SOC
17-2031.00

OVERVIEW

Biomedical engineers are highly trained scientists who use engineering and life science principles to research biological aspects of animal and human life. They develop new theories, and they modify, test, and prove existing theories on life systems. They design health care instruments and devices or apply engineering principles to the study of human systems. There are approximately 7,130 biomedical engineers employed in the United States.

HISTORY

Biomedical engineering is one of many new professions created by advancements in technology. It is an interdisciplinary field that brings together two respected professions: biology and engineering.

Biology, of course, is the study of life, and engineering, in broad terms, studies sources of energy in nature and the properties of matter in a way that is useful to humans, particularly in machines, products, and structures. A combination of the two fields, biomedical engineering developed primarily after 1945, as new technology allowed for the application of engineering principles to biology. The artificial heart is just one in a long list of the products of biomedical engineering. Other products include artificial organs, prosthetics, the use of lasers in surgery, cryosurgery, and ultrasonics, and the use of computers and thermography in diagnosis.

THE JOB

Using engineering principles to solve medical and health-related problems, the biomedical engineer works closely with life scientists, members of the medical profession, and chemists. Most of the work revolves around the laboratory. There are three interrelated work areas: research, design, and teaching.

Biomedical research is multifaceted and broad in scope. It calls upon engineers to apply their knowledge of mechanical, chemical, and electrical engineering as well as anatomy and physiology in the study of living systems. Using computers, biomedical engineers use their knowledge of graphic and related technologies to develop mathematical models that simulate physiological systems.

In biomedical engineering design, medical instruments and devices are developed. Engineers work on artificial organs, ultrasonic imagery devices, cardiac pacemakers, and surgical lasers, for example. They design and build systems that will update hospital, laboratory, and clinical procedures. They also train health care personnel in the proper use of this new equipment.

Biomedical engineering is taught on the university level. Teachers conduct classes, advise students, serve on academic committees, and supervise or conduct research.

Within biomedical engineering, an individual may concentrate on a particular specialty area. Some of the well-established specialties are *bioinstrumentation, biomechanics, biomaterials, systems physiology, clinical engineering,* and *rehabilitation engineering.* These specialty areas frequently depend on one another.

Biomechanics is mechanics applied to biological or medical problems. Examples include the artificial heart, the artificial kidney, and the artificial hip. *Biomaterials* is the study of the optimal materials with which to construct such devices, *bioinstrumentation* is the science of measuring physiological functions. *Systems physiology* uses engineering strategies, techniques, and tools to gain a comprehensive and integrated understanding of living organisms ranging from bacteria to humans. Biomedical engineers in this specialty examine such things as the biochemistry of metabolism and the control of limb movements.

Rehabilitation engineering is a new and growing specialty area of biomedical engineering. Its goal is to expand the capabilities and improve the quality of life for individuals with physical impairments. Rehabilitation engineers often work directly with the disabled person and modify equipment for individual use.

REQUIREMENTS

High School

You can best prepare for a career as a biomedical engineer by taking courses in biology, chemistry, physics, mathematics, drafting, and

computers. Communication and problem-solving skills are necessary, so classes in English, writing, and logic are important.
Participating in science clubs and competing in science fairs will give
you the opportunity to design and invent systems and products.

Postsecondary Training

Most biomedical engineers have an undergraduate degree in biomedical engineering or a related field and a Ph.D. in some facet of
biomedical engineering. Undergraduate study is roughly divided
into halves. The first two years are devoted to theoretical subjects,
such as abstract physics and differential equations in addition to the
core curriculum most undergraduates take. The third and fourth
years include more applied science. Worldwide, there are over 80
colleges and universities that offer programs in biomedical engineering.

During graduate programs, students work on research or product
development projects headed by faculty.

Certification or Licensing

Engineers whose work may affect the life, health, or safety of the public must be registered according to regulations in all 50 states and the
District of Columbia. Applicants for registration must have received
a degree from an American Board for Engineering and Technology-
accredited engineering program and have four years of experience.
They must also pass a written examination administered by the state
in which they wish to work.

Other Requirements

You should have a strong commitment to learning if you plan on
becoming a biomedical engineer. You should be scientifically inclined
and be able to apply that knowledge in problem solving. Becoming
a biomedical engineer requires long years of schooling because a biomedical engineer needs to be an expert in the fields of engineering and
biology. Also, biomedical engineers have to be familiar with chemical, material, and electrical engineering as well as physiology and
computers.

EXPLORING

Undergraduate courses offer a great deal of exposure to the field.
Working in a hospital where biomedical engineers are employed can
also provide you with insight into the field, as can interviews with
practicing or retired biomedical engineers.

EMPLOYERS

There are approximately 7,130 biomedical engineers working in the United States. About 30 percent are employed by industry, mainly industry involving the manufacture of medical supplies and instruments. In addition, many biomedical engineers are employed in hospitals and medical institutions, and in research and educational facilities. Employment opportunities also exist in government regulatory agencies.

STARTING OUT

A variety of routes may be taken to gain employment as a biomedical engineer. Recent graduates may use college placement services, or they may apply directly to employers, often to personnel offices in hospitals and industry. A job may be secured by answering an advertisement in the employment section of a newspaper. Information on job openings is also available at the local office of the U.S. Employment Service.

ADVANCEMENT

Advancement opportunities are tied directly to educational and research background. In a nonteaching capacity, a biomedical engineer with an advanced degree can rise to a supervisory position. In teaching, a doctorate is usually necessary to become a full professor. By demonstrating excellence in research, teaching, and departmental committee involvement, one can move from instructor to assistant professor and then to full professor, department chair, or even dean.

Qualifying for and receiving research grant funding can also be a means of advancing one's career in both the nonteaching and teaching sectors.

EARNINGS

The amount a biomedical engineer earns is dependent upon education, experience, and type of employer. According to the U.S. Department of Labor, biomedical engineers had a median yearly income of $60,410 in 2002. At the low end of the pay scale, 10 percent earned less than $38,250 per year, and at the high end, 10 percent earned more than $94,270 annually.

According to a 2003 survey by the National Association of Colleges and Employers, the average beginning salary for those with

Words to Know

Bioinstrumentation: Building machines for the diagnosis and treatment of disease.

Biomaterials: Anything that replaces natural tissue. These can be artificial materials or living tissues grown for implantation.

Biomechanics: Developing mechanical devices like the artificial hip, heart, and kidney.

Cellular, tissue, and genetic engineering: Application of engineering at the cellular and subcellular level to study diseases and design intervention techniques.

Clinical engineering: Application of engineering to health care through customizing and maintaining sophisticated medical equipment.

Systems physiology: Using engineering principles to understand how living systems operate.

bachelor's degrees in biological sciences was between $23,000 and $35,000 per year.

The American Association of University Professors reports that assistant professors who teach in the top paying disciplines (which includes health professions and engineering) earned an average of $58,576 for 2003. Those who were full professors earned an average of $100,682 during that same period.

Biomedical engineers can expect benefits from employers, including health insurance, paid vacation and sick days, and retirement plans.

WORK ENVIRONMENT

Biomedical engineers who teach in a university will have much student contact in the classroom, the laboratory, and the office. They also will be expected to serve on relevant committees while continuing their teaching, research, and writing responsibilities. As competition for teaching positions increases, the requirement that professors publish papers will increase. Professors usually are responsible for obtaining government or private research grants to support their work.

Those who work in industry and government have much contact with other professionals, including chemists, medical scientists, and doctors. They often work as part of a team, testing and developing new products. All biomedical engineers who do lab work are in clean, well-lighted environments, using sophisticated equipment.

OUTLOOK

It is expected that there will be a greater need for skilled biomedical engineers in the future. Prospects look particularly good in the health care industry, which will continue to grow rapidly, primarily because people are living longer. The U.S. Department of Labor predicts employment for biomedical engineers to increase faster than the average through 2012. New jobs will become available in biomedical research in prosthetics, artificial internal organs, computer applications, and instrumentation and other medical systems. In addition, a demand will exist for professors to train the biomedical engineers needed to fill these positions.

FOR MORE INFORMATION

For more information on careers in biomedical engineering, contact
American Society for Engineering Education
1818 N Street, NW, Suite 600
Washington, DC 20036
Tel: 202-331-3500
http://www.asee.org

For information on careers, student chapters, and to read the brochure Planning a Career in Biomedical Engineering, *contact or visit the following website:*
Biomedical Engineering Society
8401 Corporate Drive, Suite 225
Landover, MD 20785-2224
Tel: 301-459-1999
Email: info@bmes.org
http://www.bmes.org

For information on high school programs that provide opportunities to learn about engineering technology, contact JETS.
Junior Engineering Technical Society (JETS)
1420 King Street, Suite 405
Alexandria, VA 22314
Tel: 703-548-5387
Email: jetsinfo@jets.org
http://www.jets.org

For Canadian career information, contact
Canadian Medical and Biological Engineering Society
PO Box 51023
Orleans, ON K1E 3W4 Canada
Tel: 613-837-8649
Email: cmbes@magma.ca
http://www.cmbes.ca

Visit the following website for more information on educational programs, job listings, grants, and links to other biomedical engineering sites:
The Biomedical Engineering Network
http://www.bmenet.org

Botanists

OVERVIEW

Botanists study all different aspects of plant life, from cell structure to reproduction, to how plants are distributed, to how rainfall or other conditions affect them, and more. Botany is an integral part of modern science and industry, with diverse applications in agriculture, agronomy (soil and crop science), conservation, manufacturing, forestry, horticulture, and other areas. Botanists work for the government, in research and teaching institutions, and for private industry. The primary task of botanists is research and applied research. Nonresearch jobs in testing and inspection, or as lab technicians/technical assistants, also are available. Botany is an extremely diverse field with many specialties.

HISTORY

Plant science is hundreds of years old. The invention of microscopes in the 1600s was very important to the development of modern botany. Microscopes allowed minute study of plant anatomy and cells and led to considerable research in the field. It was in the 1600s that people started using words like *botanographist* or *botanologist,* for one who describes plants.

In the 1700s, Carolus Linnaeus, a Swedish botanist and *taxonomist* (one who identifies, names, and classifies plants) was an important figure. He came up with the two-name (genus and species) system for describing plants that is still used today. In all, Linnaeus wrote more than 180 works on plants, plant diseases, and related subjects.

In Austria during the 19th century, the first experiments in hybridization were done by a monk, Gregor Johann Mendel. He experimented on garden peas and other plants to figure out why organisms inherit the traits they do. His work is the basis for 20th and 21st century work in plant and animal genetics. As interest in botany grew, botanical gardens became popular in Europe and North America.

Botany is a major branch of biology; the other is zoology. Today, studies in botany reach into many areas of biology, including genetics, biophysics, and other specialized studies. It has taken on particular urgency as a potential source of help for creating new drugs to fight disease, meeting food needs of developing countries, and battling environmental problems.

THE JOB

Research and applied research are the primary tasks of botanists. Literally every aspect of plant life is studied: cell structure, anatomy, heredity, reproduction, and growth; how plants are distributed on the earth; how rainfall, climate, soil, elevation, and other conditions affect plants; and how humans can put plants to better use. In most cases, botanists work at a specific problem or set of problems in their research. For example, they may develop new varieties of crops that will better resist disease. Some botanists focus on a specific type of plant species, such as fungi (mycology), or plants that are native to a specific area, such as a forest or prairie. A botanist working in private industry, for example, for a food or drug company, may focus on new-product development, testing and inspection, regulatory compliance, or other areas.

Research takes place in laboratories, experiment stations (research sites found at many universities), botanical gardens, and other facilities. Powerful microscopes and special mounting, staining, and preserving techniques may be used in the research.

Some botanists, particularly those working in conservation or ecological areas, also go out into the field. They inventory species, help recreate lost or damaged ecosystems, or direct pollution cleanup efforts.

Nonresearch jobs in testing and inspection or as lab technicians/technical assistants for universities, museums, government agencies, parks, manufacturing companies, botanical gardens, and other facilities also are available.

Botany is an extremely diverse field with many specialties. *Ethnobotanists* study the use of plant life by a particular culture, people, or ethnic group to find medicinal uses of certain plants. Study of traditional Native American medicinal uses of plants is an example.

Botanist Charles T. Bryson clips tropical soda apple *(Solanum viarum)* plants in field experiments. In the United States, the weed is found primarily in the Southeast. *(Photo by Peggy Greb/USDA)*

Forest ecologists focus on forest species and their habitats, such as forest wetlands. Related studies include forest genetics and forest economics. Jobs in forestry include work in managing, maintaining, and improving forest species and environments.

Mycologists study fungi and apply their findings in agriculture, medicine, and industry for development of drugs, medicines, molds, and yeasts. They may specialize in research and development in a field such as antibiotics.

Toxicologists study the effect of toxic substances on organisms, including plants. Results of their work may be used in regulatory action, product labeling, and other areas. (For more information, see Toxicologists.)

Other botanical specialists include *pteridologists,* who study ferns and other related plants, *bryologists,* who study mosses and similar plants, and *lichenologists,* who study lichens, which are dual organisms made of both alga and fungus.

REQUIREMENTS

High School

To prepare for a career in botany, high school students can explore their interests by taking biology, doing science projects involving plants, and working during summers or school holidays for a nursery, park, or similar operation. College prep courses in chemistry, physics, biology, mathematics, English, and foreign language are a good idea because educational requirements for professional botanists are high. Nonresearch jobs (test and inspection professionals, lab technicians, technical assistants) require at least a bachelor's degree in a biological science or botany; research and teaching positions usually require at least a master's or even a doctorate.

Postsecondary Training

At the undergraduate level, there are numerous programs for degrees in botany or biology (which includes studies in both botany and zoology). The master's level and above usually involves a specialized degree. One newer degree is conservation biology, which focuses on the conservation of specific plant and animal communities. The University of Wisconsin has one of the biggest programs in this area. Another key school is Yale's forestry school, which offers degrees in areas such as natural resource management.

Other Requirements

Botanists become botanists because of their love for plants, gardening, and nature. They need patience, an exploring spirit, the ability to work well alone or with other people, good writing and other communication skills, and tenacity.

EXPLORING

The Botanical Society of America (BSA) suggests high school students take part in science fairs and clubs and get summer jobs with parks, nurseries, farms, experiment stations, labs, camps, florists, or landscape architects. Hobbies like camping, photography, and computers are useful, too, says BSA. Tour a botanical garden in your area and talk to staff. You can also get information by contacting national associations. For example, write to the Botanical Society of America for a booklet on careers in botany.

EMPLOYERS

Botanists find employment in the government, in research and teaching institutions, and in private industry. Local, state, and federal agencies, including the Department of Agriculture, Environmental Protection Agency, Public Health Service, National Biological Service, and the National Aeronautics and Space Administration

(NASA) employ botanists. Countless colleges and universities have botany departments and conduct botanical research. In private industry, botanists work for agribusiness, biotechnology, biological supply, chemical, environmental, food, lumber and paper, pharmaceutical, and petrochemical companies. Botanists also work for greenhouses, arboretums, herbariums, seed and nursery companies, and fruit growers.

STARTING OUT

With a bachelor's degree, a botanist's first job may be as a technical assistant or technician for a lab. Those with a master's degree might get work on a university research project. Someone with a doctorate might get into research and development with a drug, pharmaceutical, or other manufacturer.

For some positions, contract work might be necessary before the botanist gains a full-time position. Contract work is work done on a per-project, or freelance, basis: You sign on for that one project, and then you move on. Conservation groups like The Nature Conservancy (TNC) hire hundreds of contract workers, including ecologists and botanists, each year to do certain work. Contract workers are especially in demand in the summer when there's a lot of biology inventory work to be done.

Opportunities for internships are available with local chapters of TNC. It's also possible to volunteer. Contact the Student Conservation Association for volunteer opportunities. (Contact information can be found at the end of this article.) Land trusts are also good places to check for volunteer work.

ADVANCEMENT

Federal employees generally move up the ranks after gaining a certain number of hours of experience and obtaining advanced degrees. The Botanical Society of America, whose membership primarily comes from universities, says keys for advancing in university positions include producing quality research, publishing a lot, and obtaining advanced degrees. Advancing in the private sector depends on the individual employer. Whatever the botanist can do to contribute to the bottom line, such as making breakthroughs in new product development, improving growing methods, and creating better test and inspection methods, will probably help the botanist advance in the company.

Profile: John Bartram (1699–1777)

John Bartram was the first native-born American botanist. Born at Marple, near Philadelphia, he became interested in botany as a child and studied the subject on his own. In 1728 he founded the first botanical gardens in North America at Kingsessing. The 27-acre tract is now a part of the Philadelphia park system.

Bartram was the first American botanist to experiment with breeding and improving plants. In search of new plants, he explored the Allegheny and Catskill mountains and made trips to Florida and the Carolinas. Famous in Europe as well as in America, he was appointed botanist to King George III of England in 1765. Bartram exchanged plants with many European botanists. The Swedish botanist Carolus Linnaeus called him the "greatest natural botanist" of his time.

EARNINGS

The U.S. Department of Labor reports that biological scientists made median annual salaries of about $61,000 a year. According to the National Association of Colleges and Employers, in 2003 graduates with a bachelor's degree in biological sciences received average starting salary offers of $29,256 a year; those with master's degrees received offers of $33,600, and those with Ph.D.'s received offers of $42,244. Biological scientists working for the federal government earned average salaries of $66,200 a year in 2003, with some making more than $90,000.

At times, research botanists deeply involved with a project put in a lot of overtime. In exchange, they may be able to work fewer hours other weeks, depending on the specific employer. Botanists performing fieldwork also might have some flexibility of hours. In private industry, the workweek is likely to be a standard 35 to 40 hours. Benefits vary but usually include paid holidays and vacations, and health insurance.

WORK ENVIRONMENT

Botanists work in a wide variety of settings, some of them very pleasant: greenhouses, botanical gardens, and herbariums, for example. A botanist working for an environmental consultant or conservation organization may spend a lot of time outdoors, rain or shine. Some botanists interact with the public, such as in a public park or greenhouse, sharing their enthusiasm for the field. Other botanists spend their days in a lab, poring over specimens and writing up the results of their research.

As scientists, botanists need to be focused, patient, and determined. Some research spans many hours and even years of work. A botanist needs to believe in what he or she is doing and keep at a project until it's completed satisfactorily. The ability to work on one's own is important, but few scientists work in a vacuum. They cooperate with others, share the results of their work orally and in writing, and, particularly in private industry, may need to explain what they're doing in layman's terms.

OUTLOOK

Employment growth at a rate about as fast as the average for all biological scientists, including botanists, is expected through 2012, according to the U.S. Department of Labor. Botanists will be needed to help meet growing environmental, conservation, pharmaceutical, and similar demands. However, budget cuts and a large number of graduates have made competition for jobs strong. Government employment opportunities should stay strong, but will depend in part on the continued health of the national economy. Federal budget cuts may jeopardize some projects and positions. Experts say the outlook is best for those with an advanced degree.

FOR MORE INFORMATION

For the booklets Careers in Botany *and* Botany for the Next Millennium, *contact*
Botanical Society of America
4475 Castleman Avenue
PO Box 299
St. Louis, MO 63166-0299
Tel: 314-577-9566
Email: bsa-manager@botany.org
http://www.botany.org

For information on school and internship programs, news on endangered species, and membership information, contact
National Wildlife Federation
11100 Wildlife Center Drive
Reston, VA 20190-5362
Tel: 800-822-9919
http://www.nwf.org

For information about internships with state chapters or at TNC headquarters, contact
The Nature Conservancy (TNC)
4245 North Fairfax Drive, Suite 100
Arlington, VA 22203-1606
Tel: 800-628-6860
Email: comment@tnc.org
http://nature.org

To learn about volunteer positions in natural resource management, contact
Student Conservation Association
689 River Road
PO Box 550
Charlestown, NH 03603
Tel: 603-543-1700
Email: ask-us@sca-inc.org
http://www.sca-inc.org

This government agency manages more than 450 national wildlife refuges. The service's website has information on volunteer opportunities, careers, and answers to many frequently asked questions.
U.S. Fish and Wildlife Service
U.S. Department of the Interior
1849 C Street, NW
Washington, DC 20240
Email: contact@fws.gov
http://www.fws.gov

Cytotechnologists

OVERVIEW

Cytotechnologists are laboratory specialists who study cells under microscopes, searching for cell abnormalities such as changes in color, shape, or size that might indicate the presence of disease. Cytotechnologists may also assist physicians in the collection of body cells from various body sites, prepare slides, keep records, file reports, and consult with coworkers and pathologists. Most cytotechnologists work in private medical laboratories or in the laboratories of hospitals or research institutions.

HISTORY

The cytotechnology field is only a half-century old. It began in the 1940s, more than 10 years after Dr. George N. Papanicolaou, a Greek-American physician, developed a procedure for early diagnosis of cancer of the cervix in 1928, now known as the "Pap smear." This test involved collecting cell samples by scraping the cervixes of female patients, placing them on glass slides, staining them, and examining them under a microscope to detect cell differences and abnormalities. As the value of the test became more widely accepted, the demand for trained personnel to read the Pap smears grew, and the career of cytotechnologist was born. This field has expanded to include the examination of other cell specimens.

QUICK FACTS

School Subjects
Biology
Chemistry

Personal Skills
Helping/teaching
Technical/scientific

Work Environment
Primarily indoors
Primarily one location

Minimum Education Level
Bachelor's degree

Salary Range
$31,410 to $44,460 to
$60,790

Certification or Licensing
Required by certain states

Outlook
About as fast as the average

DOT
078

GOE
14.05.01

NOC
3211

O*NET-SOC
29-2011.00

THE JOB

Cytotechnologists primarily examine prepared slides of body cells by viewing them through a microscope. In any single slide there may be

Preparing a Slide

To prepare a slide, cells are spread, or "fixed," in the center of narrow glass rectangles. Following this, colored dye is added to emphasize cell structure and make disease detection easier. Finally, using a smaller piece of glass, the specimens are covered and sealed in order to preserve them.

more than 100,000 cells, so it is important that cytotechnologists be patient, thorough, and accurate when performing their job. They are required to study the slides and examine cell growth patterns, looking for abnormal patterns or changes in a cell's color, shape, or size that might indicate the presence of disease.

While most cytotechnologists spend the majority of their workday in the laboratory, some might assist doctors at patients' bedsides collecting cell samples from the respiratory and urinary systems, as well as the gastrointestinal tract. They might also assist physicians with bronchoscopes and with needle aspirations, a process that uses very fine needles to suction cells from many locations within the body. Once the cells are collected, cytotechnologists may prepare the slides for microscope examination. In some laboratories, cell preparation is done by medical technicians known as *cytotechnicians.*

Cytotechnologists are often responsible for keeping records and filing reports. Although they usually work independently in the lab, they often share lab space and must consult with coworkers, supervisors, and pathologists regarding their findings. Most cytotechnologists work for private firms that are hired by physicians to evaluate medical tests, but they may also work for hospitals or university research institutions.

REQUIREMENTS

High School
Biology, chemistry, and other science courses are essential if you want to become a cytotechnologist. In addition, math, English, and computer literacy classes are also important. You should also take the courses necessary to fulfill the entrance requirements of the college or university you plan to attend.

Postsecondary Training
There are two options for becoming a cytotechnologist. The first involves earning a bachelor's degree in biology, life sciences, or a relat-

ed field, then entering a one-year, postbaccalaureate certificate program offered by an accredited hospital or university.

The second option involves transferring into a cytotechnology program during your junior or senior year of college. Students on this track earn a bachelor of science degree in cytotechnology. In both cases, you would earn a college degree and complete at least one year of training devoted to cytotechnology.

The courses you will take include chemistry, biology, and math. Some programs also require their students to take business and computer classes as well.

Certification or Licensing

Cytotechnology graduates (from either degree programs or certificate programs) may register for the certification examination given by the Board of Registry of the American Society of Clinical Pathologists. Most states require cytotechnologists to be certified, and most employers insist that new employees be certified. Certification is usually a requirement for advancement in the field.

A number of states also require that personnel working in laboratories be licensed. It will be necessary for you to check the licensing requirements of the state in which you hope to work. The state's department of health or board of occupational licensing can provide you with this information.

It is important that practicing cytotechnologists remain current with new ideas, techniques, and medical discoveries. Many continuing education programs are offered to help the professional remain current in the field of cytotechnology.

Other Requirements

If you wish to enter the field of cytotechnology you should be detail-oriented, a good observer, and able to make decisions. You should enjoy working alone, but you must also have the ability to work as a team member. It is essential that you are able to follow directions and have the ability to concentrate. Good writing, reporting, and organizational skills are also important. Cytotechnologists are often expected to sit at a stationary laboratory bench for long periods of time.

EXPLORING

"If you like to work jigsaw puzzles, cytotechnology just might be the career for you," suggests Susan Dingler, cytotechnologist at the School of Cytotechnology at Henry Ford Hospital in Detroit. "Like jigsaw puzzle fans, cytotechnologists enjoy comparing the shapes and sizes of small objects, scanning a lot of similar objects as they try to detect subtle differences. Both puzzles and microscope work require hard concentration, patience, and observation of acute detail."

Participate in science clubs and competitions that help you become familiar with microscopes and allow you to practice making slides. Ask a science teacher or guidance counselor to help you contact museums that are involved in research. These museums may let students view slide collections and see what goes on behind the scenes.

Volunteer or apply for part-time work at hospitals or independent laboratories to get experience in health care settings.

EMPLOYERS

The majority of cytotechnologists are employed by private medical laboratories hired by physicians to evaluate medical tests. Others work for hospitals, nursing homes, public health facilities, or university research institutions, while some may be employed by federal and state governments.

STARTING OUT

Some universities and teaching hospitals have internship programs that can result in job offers upon graduation. Recruiters often visit universities and teaching hospitals in the months prior to a graduation in an effort to recruit cytotechnologists. Professional journals and large metropolitan newspapers often have classified ads that list opportunities for employment. Many university and teaching hospitals have a placement service that helps their graduates obtain employment upon graduation.

ADVANCEMENT

Some cytotechnologists who work in larger labs may advance to supervisory positions. This type of advancement may be limited in smaller labs, however. Entering the teaching field and directing classes or supervising research may be another career advancement move. Some experienced cytotechnologists, along with other medical personnel, have opened their own laboratories. Obtaining additional education or training can open the door to other careers in the medical field.

EARNINGS

Salaries are determined by the experience and education of the cytotechnologist and by the type and size of employer. For example, federal government employees are generally paid a lower salary than those working in the private sector, and cytotechnologists working in private laboratories earn slightly more than those working in hospitals. Salaries tend to be higher in the west.

The U.S. Department of Labor reports the median yearly income of medical and clinical laboratory technologists (a group including cytotechnologists) as $44,460 in 2003. The lowest paid 10 percent, which typically includes those just beginning in the field, earned less than $31,410. The highest paid 10 percent made more than $60,790 annually.

Benefits such as vacation time, sick leave, insurance, and other fringe benefits vary by employer, but are usually consistent with other full-time health care workers.

WORK ENVIRONMENT

Cytotechnologists usually work independently in a well-lighted laboratory examining slides under the microscope. Often this involves sitting at a workstation for a considerable length of time and requires intense concentration. Some cytotechnologists might assist other medical personnel with the direct collection of cell samples from patients. This type of work requires interacting directly with people who are ill or who may be concerned about their health and the test results. Cytotechnologists do not necessarily work nine-to-five hours. Daily schedules and shifts may vary according to the size of the laboratory and medical facility.

OUTLOOK

Competition to enter cytotechnology programs is keen, and there is also strong competition among graduates for the best jobs. The U.S. Department of Labor predicts employment for all medical and clinical technologists to grow about as fast as the average through 2012. Advances in technology have made many new diagnostic tests possible, but advances in technology have also caused much automation to take place in the laboratory. So, while there are new tests for the cytotechnologist to perform, there are also fewer old tests that need the cytotechnologist's expert handling. However, it is important to note that government regulations currently limit the number of slides cytotechnologists may work with each day, adding to demand for workers in this field.

FOR MORE INFORMATION

For information on cytotechnology careers, accredited schools, and employment opportunities, contact the following organizations:

American Society for Cytotechnology
1500 Sunday Drive, Suite 102
Raleigh, NC 27607
Tel: 800-948-3947
Email: info@asct.com
http://www.asct.com

American Society of Clinical Pathologists
2100 West Harrison Street
Chicago, IL 60612
Tel: 312-738-1336
Email: info@ascp.org
http://www.ascp.org

American Society of Cytopathology
400 West 9th Street, Suite 201
Wilmington, DE 19801
Tel: 302-429-8802
http://www.cytopathology.org

Commission on Accreditation of Allied Health Education Programs
35 East Wacker Drive, Suite 1970
Chicago, IL 60601-2208
Tel: 312-553-9355
Email: caahep@caahep.org
http://www.caahep.org

Ecologists

OVERVIEW

Ecology is the study of the interconnections between organisms (plants, animals) and the physical environment. It links biology, which includes both zoology (the study of animals) and botany (the study of plants), with physical sciences such as geology and paleontology. Thus, *ecologist* is a broad name for any of a number of different biological or physical scientists concerned with the study of plants or animals within their environment.

HISTORY

Much of the science that ecologists use is not new. The ancient Greeks recorded their observations of natural history many centuries ago. However, linking together the studies of life and the physical environment is fairly new. The term "ecology" was first defined in 1866 by Ernst von Haeckel, a German biologist. Like many scientists of his time, he grappled with Charles Darwin's theory of evolution based on natural selection. This theory said that those species of plants and animals that were best adapted to their environment would survive. Although Haeckel did not agree with Darwin, he and many other scientists grew fascinated with the links between living things and their physical environment. At that time, very important discoveries in geology proved that many forms of plants and animals had once existed but had died out. Fossils showed startlingly unfamiliar plant types, for example, as well as prehistoric animal remains that no one had ever imagined existed. (Before such discoveries, people assumed that the species they saw all around them had always existed.) Realization that there were important connections between living things and their physical environment was a key step in the development of the science of ecology.

Like most of the other environmental careers, the professional field of ecology did not really grow popular until the late 1960s and early 1970s. Before then, some scientists and others had tried to warn the public about the ill effects of industrialization, unchecked natural resource consumption, overpopulation, spoiling of wilderness areas, and other thoughtless misuse of the environment. But not until the years after World War II (with growing use of radiation and of pesticides and other chemicals, soaring industrial and automobile pollution, and increasing discharge into waterways) did widespread public alarm about the environment grow. By this time, many feared it was too late. Heavy municipal and industrial discharge into Lake Erie, for example, made it unable to sustain life as before.

In response, the U.S. government passed a series of hard-hitting environmental laws during the 1960s and 1970s. To become compliant with these laws, companies and municipalities began to look around for professionals who understood the problems and could help take steps to remedy them. Originally, they drew professionals from many existing fields, such as geologists, sanitary engineers, biologists and chemists. These professionals may not have studied environmental problems as such at school, but they were able to apply the science they knew to the problems at hand.

To some extent, this continues to be true today. Many people working on environmental problems still come from general science or engineering backgrounds. Recently, however, there has been a trend toward specialization. Students in fields such as biology, chemistry, engineering, law, urban planning, and communications can obtain degrees with specialization in the environment. An ecologist today can either have a background in traditional biological or physical sciences or have studied these subjects specifically in the context of environmental problems.

THE JOB

The main unit of study in ecology is the ecosystem. Ecosystems are communities of plants and animals within a given habitat that provide the necessary means of survival, including food and water. Ecosystems are defined by such physical conditions as climate, altitude, latitude, and soil and water characteristics. Examples include forests, tundra, savannas (grasslands), and rainforests.

There are many complex and delicate interrelationships within an ecosystem. For example, green plants use the energy of sunlight to make carbohydrates, fats, and proteins; some animals eat these plants and acquire part of the energy of the carbohydrates, fats, and proteins; other animals eat these animals and acquire a smaller part of that energy. Cycles of photosynthesis, respiration, and nitrogen fixation continuously recycle the chemicals of life needed to support the ecosystem. Anything that disrupts these cycles, such as droughts, or the pollution of air or water, can disrupt the delicate workings of the entire ecosystem.

Therefore, a primary concern of ecologists today is to study and attempt to find solutions for disruptions in various ecosystems. Increasingly, an area of expertise is the reconstruction of ecosystems—that is, the restoration of ecosystems that are destroyed or almost completely destroyed because of pollution, overuse of land, or other action.

According to the Environmental Careers Organization, a key area of work for ecologists is in land and water conservation. They help to restore damaged land and water as well as to preserve wild areas for the future. Understanding the links between organisms and their physical environments can be invaluable in such efforts.

For example, imagine that there is a large pond at the edge of a town. A woman out jogging one day notices that hundreds of small, dead fish have washed up at the edge of the pond; a "fish kill," in environmental language. Clearly, something is wrong, but what? A nearby factory discharges its wastewater into the pond. Is there something new in the wastewater that killed the fish? Or did something else kill the fish? A professional who understands the fish, the habitat (the pond), the possible reasons for the fish kill, and the potential solutions clearly would be useful here.

This is also true for environmental planning and resource management. Planning involves studying and reporting the impact of an action on the environment. For example, how might the construction of a new federal highway affect the surrounding ecosystem? A planning team may go to the site to view the physical geography and environment, the plants, and the animals. It also may recommend alternative actions that will have less damaging effects.

Resource management means determining what resources already exist and working to use them wisely. Professionals may build databases cataloging the plants, animals, and physical characteristics of a given area. They also may report on what can be done to ensure that the ecosystem can continue to sustain itself in the future. If an ecosystem has been completely destroyed, ecologists can help reconstruct it, getting the physical environment back up to par and reintroducing the species that used to live there.

Ecologist Ray Carruthers measures plant and flower head density of yellow starthistle while technician Justin Weber uses a sweep net to sample populations of biocontrol agent *Chaetorellia succinea*. *(Photo by Peggy Greb/USDA)*

Ecologists work in many areas of specialization. *Limnologists* study freshwater ecology; *hydrogeologists* focus on water on or below the surface of the earth; *paleontologists* study the remains of ancient life-forms in the form of fossils; *geomorphologists* study the origin of landforms and their changes; and *geochemists* study the chemistry of the earth, including the effect of pollution on the earth's chemistry. Other specialties are those of the endangered species biologists and wetlands ecologists.

REQUIREMENTS

High School

If you are interested in becoming an ecologist, you should take a college preparatory curriculum while in high school. Classes that will be of particular benefit include earth science, biology, chemistry, English, and math. Because computers are so often involved in various aspects of research and documentation, you should also take computer science courses.

Postsecondary Training

A bachelor of science degree is the minimum degree required for nonresearch jobs, which include testing and inspection. A master's degree is necessary for jobs in applied research or management. A Ph.D. generally is required to advance in the field, including into administrative positions.

The Environmental Careers Organization suggests that if you can only take one undergraduate major, it should be in the basic sciences: biology, botany, zoology, chemistry, physics, or geology. At the master's degree level, natural resource management, ecology, botany, conservation biology, and forestry studies are useful.

Certification or Licensing

The Ecological Society of America offers professional certification at three levels: associate ecologist, ecologist, and senior ecologist. A candidate's certification level will depend on the amount of education and professional experience he or she has. The society encourages certification as a way to enhance ecologists' professional standing in society.

Other Requirements

Ecologists should appreciate and respect nature, and they must also be well versed in scientific fundamentals. Ecologists frequently, but not always, are naturally idealistic. They should be able to work with other people on a team and to express their special knowledge to the other people on the team, who may have different areas of specialization.

EXPLORING

You can seek more information about ecology from guidance counselors and professional ecologists who work at nearby colleges, universities, and government agencies. An easy way for you to learn more about ecology is to study your own environment. Trips to a nearby pond, forest, or park over the course of several months will provide opportunities to observe and collect data. Science teachers and local park service or arboretum personnel can also offer you guidance.

EMPLOYERS

By far, the majority of land and water conservation jobs (about 75 percent) are in the public sector, according to the Environmental Careers Organization. This includes the federal government, the largest employer. The Bureau of Land Management, the U.S. Fish and Wildlife Service, the National Park Service, and the U.S. Geological Service are among the federal agencies that manage U.S. conservation.

Other public sector opportunities are with states, regions, and towns. Opportunities in the private sector can be found with utilities, timber companies, and consulting firms. An additional area of employment is in teaching.

STARTING OUT

Internships provide an excellent point of entry into this field. You can volunteer with such groups as the Student Conservation Association (SCA), which places people in resource management projects. Programs include three- to five-week summer internships for high school students. If you have already graduated from high school (and are over age 18), you can check with SCA for internships in forest, wildlife, resource, and other agencies.

Another option is to contact a federal or local government agency directly about an internship. Many, including the Environmental Protection Agency, National Park Service, and Bureau of Land Management, have internship programs. Programs are more informal at the local level.

As for the private sector, an internship with a nonprofit organization may be possible. Such groups include the National Wildlife Federation and the Natural Resources Defense Council.

Entry-level ecologists also may take advantage of temporary or seasonal jobs to gain experience and establish crucial contacts in the field.

ADVANCEMENT

Mid-level biological scientists may move to managerial positions within biology or to nontechnical administrative, sales, or managerial jobs. Ecologists with a Ph.D. may conduct independent research, advance into administrative positions, or teach on the college level, advancing from assistant professor to associate and tenured professorships.

EARNINGS

In 2003, the U.S. Department of Labor reported the median annual income of zoologists and wildlife biologists was $49,320, with the lowest 10 percent of this group earning less than $31,070 and the highest 10 percent earning more than $76,600. Ecologists working for the federal government in 2003 earned average salaries of $65,207. Federal agency jobs tend to pay more than state or local agency jobs. Private sector jobs tend to pay more than public sector jobs.

WORK ENVIRONMENT

Ecologists can work in a variety of places, from wilderness areas to forests to mountain streams. Ecologists also might work in sewage treatment plants, spend their days in front of computers or in research laboratories, or find themselves testifying in court. A certain amount of idealism probably is useful, though not required. It takes more than just loving nature to be in this field; a person has to be good at scientific fundamentals. Ecologists might start out in the field collecting samples, making notes about animal habits, or doing other monitoring. They may need to be able to work as part of a team and express what they know in terms that everyone on the team can understand.

OUTLOOK

Environmentally oriented jobs are expected to increase at a faster rate than the average for all occupations through 2012, according to the U.S. Department of Labor. Land and resource conservation jobs tend to be the most scarce, however, because of high popularity and tight budgets for such agencies. Those with advanced degrees will fare better than ecologists with only bachelor's degrees.

FOR MORE INFORMATION

For information on careers in the geosciences, contact
American Geological Institute
4220 King Street
Alexandria, VA 22302-1502
Tel: 703-379-2480
http://www.agiweb.org

In addition to certification, ESA offers a wide variety of publications, including Issues in Ecology, *and fact sheets about specific ecological concerns. For more information contact*
Ecological Society of America (ESA)
1707 H Street, NW, Suite 400
Washington, DC 20006
Tel: 202-833-8773
Email: esahq@esa.org
http://esa.org

For information on paid internships and careers in the field, contact
Environmental Careers Organization
30 Winter Street
Boston, MA 02108
Tel: 617-426-4375
http://www.eco.org

For information on internships, job opportunities, and student chapters, contact
National Wildlife Federation
11100 Wildlife Center Drive
Reston, VA 20190-5362
Tel: 703-438-6000
http://www.nwf.org

For information on student volunteer activities and programs, contact
Student Conservation Association
689 River Road
PO Box 550
Charlestown, NH 03603
Tel: 603-543-1700
Email: ask-us@sca-inc.org
http://www.thesca.org

Ethnoscientists

OVERVIEW

Ethnoscientist is a broad term that covers various specialties, such as ethnoarchaeology, ethnobiology, ethnomusicology, ethnoveterinary medicine, and ethnozoology. Ethnoscientists study a particular subject, usually a social or life science, (e.g., archaeology, biology, veterinary medicine, or zoology) from the perspective of one or more cultural groups.

Ethnoscientists are usually Western practitioners who are interested in exploring the knowledge, beliefs, traditions, and practices of cultures in non-industrialized areas of the world, such as the Maoris of New Zealand, the Shona of south-central Africa, or the Inuit of Alaska. These cultures have unique, often undocumented, ways of perceiving, interacting with, and understanding each other and their environment. Ethnoscientists study these cultures to record and learn from their perspectives.

HISTORY

Although the term is relatively new, ethnoscientific study has been around since people first began exploring the relationship between people and their environment, by studying music, language, biology, history, and all the elements that form societies and cultures.

Ethnoscience evolved as a subfield of ethnography, the study of cultural groups in the 19th century. The ethno- prefix became more widespread as the disciplines of ethnobotany, ethnobiology, and ethnoecology developed in about 1895, 1935, and 1954, respectively. Ethnohistory gained popularity in the 1930s and 1940s. Eugene Hunn, an anthropology professor with a specialization in ethnobiology at the

QUICK FACTS

School Subjects
Biology
Foreign language
History
Sociology

Personal Skills
Communication/ideas
Technical/scientific

Work Environment
Indoors and outdoors
Primarily multiple locations

Minimum Education Level
Doctoral degree

Salary Range
$32,790 to $65,290 to
$126,540+

Certification or Licensing
None available

Outlook
About as fast as the average

DOT
N/A

GOE
N/A

NOC
N/A

O*NET-SOC
N/A

University of Washington, says, "The term 'ethnobotany' was first used to refer to museum studies of native peoples' uses of plants."

"Ethnoscience was a common label in the 1960s and 1970s for a particular focus in anthropology," Hunn continues. "This has evolved into cognitive anthropology, an emphasis within sociocultural anthropology and linguistic anthropology that focuses on cultural knowledge systems, particularly their linguistic expression."

Regarding the background of ethnoveterinary medicine, Evelyn Mathias, an independent consultant focusing on integrated livestock development, comments that interest in indigenous knowledge and ethnoveterinary medicine arose with the failure of many development projects that had regarded Western technology and approaches as superior and tried to use them in other cultures with little adaptation and modification. "Over the last two or three decades, it became increasingly obvious that this type of development is inappropriate and not sustainable. Scientists and development professionals have come to realize that local people's knowledge is a valuable resource for development and they have started to study and use it in projects."

Sound-recording devices, beginning with the phonograph, have enabled ethnoscientists to record and keep sounds, such as language (ethnolinguists) and music (ethnomusicologists). More recent innovations include multimedia technology, which, according to Hunn, "is being used more frequently to present the complex data of ethnobiology, which often must include images of plants and animals, recordings of sounds of animals, recordings of the pronunciation of native names, video footage of processing activities, etc."

THE JOB

Ethnoscientists generally perform the same or similar duties as their counterparts in the traditional sciences, but from the perspective of the knowledge and belief systems of a particular indigenous group or culture. Not only do ethnoscientists conduct research in their particular area of study, but they immerse themselves in the culture and talk to the inhabitants to find out about, for example, the local knowledge and use (medicinally or otherwise) of plants (*ethnobotanist* or *ethnopharmacologist*), the local use of language (*ethnolinguist*), or the local use of implements, utensils, tools, or other items (*ethnoarchaeologists*). Ethnoscientists classify information based on traditional methods and concepts while at the same time drawing on linguistic and cognitive theories.

Because ethnoscientists study other cultural groups, they often have to travel to conduct their research and talk to the local peo-

Contributors to Ethnobiology and Ethnobotany

Brent Berlin (Ph.D., Stanford University, 1964) is well known for his collaborative field research in ethnobotany and medicinal plant use of the Mayans in Chiapas, Mexico, and Aguaruna ethnobiology in Peru. In 1973 he proposed "universals of ethnobotanical classification and nomenclature" that continue to guide research.

Harold Conklin (Ph.D., Yale University, 1955) wrote his dissertation on the Philippine Hanunoo tribe's knowledge of plants. His research helped define the field and establish high standards for the detailed ethnographic study of ethnobiology.

Richard Evan Schultes (Ph.D., Harvard University 1941) initiated studies of the uses of hallucinogenic plants by Native American peoples and is well known for his documentation of the sophisticated knowledge Amazonian Indian tribes had of the chemical properties of plants.

ple. Eugene Hunn says, "Summers or perhaps at other times when I can arrange to travel to do ethnobiological field research, I will go to Oaxaca, Mexico, Australia, or Alaska to visit villages where indigenous peoples still hunt, fish, gather, or farm their ancestral lands. With their permission and with their help, I collect plants, insects, and fungi, and observe birds, reptiles, and mammals— always with local guides who can explain to me what they call each organism and what importance each plant or bug might have for their lives. I spend a lot of time studying foreign languages and learning Latin names of plants and animals." It is important that ethnoscientists are not intrusive when conducting research. They must always remember that they are acting as observers rather than agents of change.

Hunn defines an *ethnobiologist* as "a scholar who studies what people in cultures around the world know about biology. Most often this means what they know about the plants and animals of their local environment. Ethnobiology includes ethnobotany (study of knowledge of local plants), ethnozoology (local animals), ethnoentomology (local insects), etc. Ethnobotany may focus on naming and classifying or on how plants are used, for example, for food, medicine, or construction materials. Ethnozoology could emphasize how animals are imagined in folklore or how domestic animals are cared for and utilized. Some ethnobiologists are archaeologists who analyze plant or animal remains for evidence of past use."

Hunn notes, "There are few, if any, jobs specifically for ethnobiologists, as it is a specialty that crosses the boundaries of typical academic disciplines." This also holds true for the other ethnosciences.

An ethnobiologist's primary duties are "to develop research proposals for funding that allow the researcher to travel to the field site for extended periods," explains Hunn. "An ethnobiologist collects voucher specimens (especially of plants, insects, fungi) in conjunction with recording the ethnographic information in the native language of the people of the community where the research takes place. There are ethical expectations that the ethnobiologist will publish his or her finding not only in academic journals and books but also in the local languages in a form readily accessible to the people of the study community and to the scholars of the host country (if outside the United States). Ethnobiologists in universities are expected to teach ethnobiology courses and to train students in ethnobiology."

In describing his typical day, Hunn reports, "Most of the time I work in my office preparing for classes, talking with students, reading other people's work, writing articles or books, sorting and analyzing my own data, and preparing grant proposals so that I can get out of the office and into the field, which is where I most like to be."

Evelyn Mathias explains ethnoveterinary medicine as the study of how people manage animal health care and production. "It covers everything herders and small farmers do and know to keep their animals healthy and productive." According to Mathias, there are two types of ethnoveterinarians. First there are the "local practitioners, such as herders, farmers, or healers, who use indigenous techniques to treat animals." And second are the "Western academics or development professionals who study and promote the use of indigenous techniques in agricultural development. Most of these are either veterinarians who are interested in traditional health care practices or anthropologists who study veterinary medicine."

Mathias's primary duties include doing laboratory research or a participatory research study in the field, collecting and summarizing literature, running a network on raising the awareness of the value of local knowledge, and doing project evaluations. Research entails documentation, laboratory and fieldwork, studying how to integrate local practices, and incorporating ethnoveterinary medicine into education programs.

Ethnobiologists and ethnoveterinarians account for only two of the many ethnoscience specialties. Given the multidisciplinary approach of the ethnosciences, there is great variance in definition, focus, and process among its many areas. But at the core of the ethnosciences is an immersion in other cultures and a desire to learn what is known, believed, and practiced by local inhabitants.

Ethnoarchaeologists explore contemporary cultural groups with the goal of understanding cultures of the past. They examine current customs and rituals, gather ancient and current artifacts, and talk to local inhabitants about their lifestyle. Based on their findings, ethnoarchaeologists hypothesize about a group's social organization and history.

Ethnobotanists study the use and classification of indigenous plants by a particular cultural group. Plants may be used as drugs, food, cosmetics, clothing, building material, or as part of religious ceremonies. Ethnobotanists also evaluate whether these plants have more widespread value outside the region, especially in the case of medicinal plants.

Many wild plants can only be grown in their native environment—the Amazon rainforest, for example. Ethnobotanists must be especially aware that taking plants from their environment affects the entire ecosystem, including its human inhabitants.

Economic botany, the study of plants that are commercially important, is closely related to ethnobotany. *Ethnopharmacologists* conduct research that is similar to that of ethnobotanists. The difference is that ethnopharmacologists study indigenous plants focusing on their medicinal value and use only. Ethnopharmacologists examine current indigenous remedies derived from either plant or animal substances and look for ways to develop new and better drugs. Both ethnobotanists and ethnopharmacologists must be sure that the intellectual property rights of the local people are observed, and that they receive a share in whatever financial returns may result from knowledge or use elsewhere of indigenous plants.

Ethnoecologists focus on the knowledge and understanding that indigenous peoples have of their local ecology—that is, how they interact with their environment and other organisms.

Ethnohistorians research the history of various cultures, such as Native Americans and other non-European peoples. They study maps, music, paintings, photography, folklore, oral tradition, ecology, archaeological sites and materials, museum collections, enduring customs, language, and place names.

Ethnolinguists examine the relationship between the language and the culture of a specific people. They study the structure of speech and modification of language. They look at how language is used to convey understanding and knowledge.

Ethnomusicologists study the music made by certain cultural groups as well as studying the musicians themselves. The process of making music, the sound of the music being made, musical instruments, what the music means to the creators and listeners, and dances or ceremonies associated with certain music all are components of ethnomusicology. In order to preserve a culture's music, ethnomusicologists usually make audio and video recordings in addition to written notation.

Ethnopsychiatrists are concerned with how indigenous peoples perceive and treat mental, emotional, or behavioral disorders of others within their own societies. *Ethnopsychologists* explore cultural influences on human behavior and mental characteristics of indigenous peoples, as well as their own theories of psychology.

No matter what the specialty, membership in professional organizations and reading scholarly journals are important aspects of an ethnoscientist's job. Mathias is a member of the German Veterinary Association, the League for Pastoral Peoples, and AGRECOL (Agricultural and Ecological Association). She comments that the latter two associations are particularly important to her "because they are interested in alternative approaches to development. This gives me the opportunity of exchanging information and getting some peer support." She continues, "It is important to stay up to date with the latest developments. I read books and scientific journals mainly on veterinary medicine in the tropics, development, indigenous knowledge, and related fields."

REQUIREMENTS

High School

Sociology courses will teach you the basics of research methods and observation techniques. If your school offers any anthropology classes, be sure to take them. Learning another foreign language can be helpful if you conduct field research. The foreign language you take in high school may not be the one you will need later, but learning a second language should make it easier for you to learn others. History and art classes will expose you to the cultures of different peoples of the world.

Biology and chemistry will be useful if you're considering ethnobiology, ethnobotany, or ethnopharmacology. Evelyn Mathias recommends an assortment of classes if you're interested in ethnoveterinary medicine: geography, cultural studies, biology, zoology, botany, and agriculture. She stresses the importance of classes that highlight the value of cultural diversity. Math and computer classes are also helpful.

Postsecondary Training

To teach at the university level, you will need a Ph.D. The particular field of study will depend on the line of work you want to enter. Anthropology classes, especially cultural anthropology, will be useful for study in just about any discipline. Classes in archaeology, linguistics, history, sociology, religion, and mythology can help prepare you to work with indigenous peoples. Some schools offer concentrations or courses in specific ethnosciences (e.g., ethnomusicology or ethnobiology).

If you want to pursue ethnoveterinary medicine, Mathias recommends getting a degree in a technical field, such as veterinary medicine, animal husbandry, biology, pharmacology, or botany, in addition to social science courses. To prepare for a career in ethnobotany, it is recommended that you get your degree in anthropology, botany, or pharmacology. Other important areas of study include chemistry, ecology, and medicine. According to Eugene Hunn, "Most professional ethnobiologists have doctoral degrees in anthropology or biology."

Consult relevant professional organizations, such as the Centre for International Ethnomedicinal Education and Research, the American Society for Ethnohistory, and the Society for Ethnomusicology, for lists of postsecondary programs in your area of interest.

Other Requirements

It is important that ethnoscientists possess an "openness and understanding for other cultures and the ability and willingness to learn from others and work with other peoples," notes Mathias. "Someone who has prejudices against other peoples and who believes that high-tech is the only solution possible" will not be suitable for this line of work. Many cultural groups of the world live lives that are far less technologically oriented than in the Western world. Ethnoscientists embrace those differences.

Ethnoscientists need a healthy curiosity and should enjoy research. They should be able to work independently and as part of a team.

Many ethnoscientists are away from home for extended periods and must be able to tolerate different climates, rustic accommodations, unusual foods, and demanding physical conditions. Adaptability is a key personality trait for ethnoscientists doing fieldwork.

EXPLORING

A fascination with birds, bugs, snakes, fish, or plants is what got many of Eugene Hunn's ethnobiological colleagues started early.

"Later they realized that they weren't just interested in the plants and animals but in how those plants and animals fit into people's lives. So they studied anthropology or linguistics to better understand the human side of the equation."

Explore extracurricular, volunteer, or part-time opportunities that will give you some background experience in your field of interest. If it's ethnobotany, look for a summer job working in a city park or with a local florist or nursery. If it's ethnoveterinary medicine, look for part-time or volunteer work at a veterinarian's office or animal shelter. To explore your interest in ethnozoology, work at a zoo. If enthnolinguistics interests you, try learning a language that is not offered at your school; for example, learn Swahili, Hawaiian, or Tagalog. To explore ethnomusicology, listen to recorded and live world music and visit museums and music stores that carry indigenous instruments. Museums offer a wealth of information on different cultures, including exhibits, reading materials, lectures, and workshops.

Take any opportunity offered you to travel, particularly to non-industrialized countries and more remote areas of the world that have been less influenced by Western culture. Explore study-abroad programs or consider volunteering with the Peace Corps to get an intense, long-term experience living in another culture.

Visit the websites of professional organizations, such as the Society of Ethnobiology, the Botanical Society of America, the American Society for Ethnohistory, and the Society for Ethnomusicology.

EMPLOYERS

Ethnoscientists work in the same places as other social and life scientists—universities, research institutes, government and non-government organizations, museums, and alternative medical firms. Sometimes ethnoscientists become independent consultants, as is the case with Evelyn Mathias.

Eugene Hunn says, "Most ethnobiologists work at universities as faculty members or researchers. Some may be employed by government agencies, for example, to advise National Park Service or Forest Service staff on issues relating to how local communities, such as Native American groups, interact with local plants and animals. They study how traditional and modern subsistence activities, such as hunting, fishing, gathering, herding, or farming, might affect protected areas. Some ethnoscientists work at museums and herbaria. A few jobs may be available in the private sector, with companies devel-

Examples of Ethnoscientific Research

- An ethnobotanist or ethnopharmacologist might compare how shamans of several tribes in the western Amazon rainforest use different preparations of the same plant to treat skin disorders.
- An ethnomusicologist might study the unusual vocalizations of the Tuva people in Siberia and make recordings and written notation to preserve music that has been traditionally passed down orally.
- An ethnolinguist might study how Swahili developed as a trade language to allow communication between local East African tribes and Arabs from the north.
- An ethnohistorian might research how the Baka Pygmy culture in central Africa has changed over time and how it has been affected by colonialization and industrialization.
- An ethnoveterinarian or ethnozoologist might study nomadic cattle-herding tribes of sub-Saharan and East Africa to learn how herders find pasture, how they avoid tsetse-infested areas, and how they prevent diseases.

oping new products modeled on how indigenous peoples use plants or animals—for example, drugs, cosmetics, or teas."

STARTING OUT

While working on your degree, be sure to communicate your interests to your professors. They may be aware of opportunities at the university or elsewhere. You might be able to participate in a university research project or become a research assistant or teaching fellow. Professional organizations are another important resource when it comes to finding a job. If you network with others in your field, you have a good chance of hearing about job opportunities. Also, organizations might post information on jobs, internships, or apprenticeships in their journals or on their websites.

There is strong competition for academic positions. Most students begin their job search while finishing their graduate degrees. Your first position is likely to be an instructor in general courses in anthropology, sociology, history, biology, or botany, depending on your specialty. In order to advance to higher ranks of professor, you will be required to do research, during which you can focus on your ethnoscience specialty. Evelyn Mathias suggests that, because research opportunities are difficult to come by, you might have to create your own opportunities, perhaps by proposing research projects.

Mathias earned a Ph.D. in veterinary medicine in Germany and then worked at an Indonesian university on a project dealing with water buffalo. She comments, "During this job, I stayed three months in a remote village. I realized that the university's research benefited small farmers little, as the technology was not appropriate for the infrastructure in remote rural areas. I later had the opportunity to do an M.Sc. in international development in the United States, which allowed me to combine courses on anthropology, international development, and veterinary science. As ethnoveterinary medicine is an interdisciplinary field that combines aspects of social and hard sciences, this mixture facilitated the start of my work in this field.

"I worked for three years as the coordinator of a regional program for the promotion of indigenous knowledge in Asia, sponsored by an international non-government organization in the Philippines," Mathias continues. "The program was part of an international network, and the focus of my work was on indigenous knowledge in general, with ethnoveterinary medicine being one important aspect."

ADVANCEMENT

Ethnoscientists advance by producing high-quality research and publishing articles or books. They might come to be known as experts in their field. They might become the head of a research project. The advancement path of ethnoscientists who teach in universities is instructor to assistant professor to associate professor to full professor. A full professor might eventually become a department head.

EARNINGS

The U.S. Department of Labor reports that the median salary of biological scientists, which includes biologists, botanists, ecologists, and zoologists, was $49,320 in 2003. Anthropologists and archaeologists had median annual earnings of $41,260 in 2003, while historians earned a median salary of $42,370. The median salary of veterinarians was $65,290 in 2003. Salaries for teachers in the biological sciences ranged from less than $32,790 for the lowest 10 percent to more than $126,540 for the highest 10 percent during that same year.

Eugene Hunn cautions, "If you want to get rich, you don't want to become an ethnobiologist. Most ethnobiologists—if they are lucky enough to get a good job at a university or museum—may earn $40,000 to $70,000 with a Ph.D. and some years of experience. Mostly we do it because it's fascinating and we get to travel a lot." Evelyn Mathias notes that the same thing is true in her field. "Unless you have the very rare dream job as a fully paid ethnoveterinarian (e.g., as a project researcher), ethnoveterinary work is chronically underpaid. Ethnoveterinary medicine is not for persons hoping to earn lots of money quickly. It is rather for solid scientists and idealists."

WORK ENVIRONMENT

Ethnoscientists in academia mainly work indoors. Their time is spent teaching, meeting with students, writing texts or grant proposals, or compiling and analyzing data. For Evelyn Mathias, the hardest parts of her job include networking and getting financial support so she can conduct fieldwork. Ethnoscientists who travel to do research on different cultural groups conduct fieldwork outdoors. When in the field, ethnoscientists encounter climates that are different from their own, such as the tropical rainforest or the Arctic tundra. Ethnoscientists must be ready to work outdoors, sometimes for long periods of time, no matter what the weather, and they must be prepared to stay in primitive living conditions.

OUTLOOK

The *Occupational Outlook Handbook* reports that employment for postsecondary teachers in general will grow faster than the average through 2012. This is largely because enrollment is expected to increase, creating a greater need for professors. Employment for social scientists is expected to grow about as fast as the average through 2012. Job growth that is as fast as the average is expected for medical and biological scientists, but scientists holding Ph.D.'s may face strong competition when trying to get basic research positions.

Eugene Hunn thinks that ethnobiology is a growing field "primarily because humanity is facing environmental and political crises that often have their roots in conflicts over how to use the earth's biological resources. Ethnobiologists document many alternative ways that people can live in harmony with the land, and so our research may help educate people about better ways to use the earth's resources." Evelyn Mathias believes that interest in ethnoveterinary medicine will grow as the limitations of modern medicine and development are becoming more obvious.

While interest may increase, it is difficult to say whether funding will increase as well. If there are federal budget cuts, there might be a decrease in the amount of money devoted to new government research projects, or existing projects might not get renewed.

FOR MORE INFORMATION

For information on careers in anthropology, contact
American Anthropological Association
2200 Wilson Boulevard, Suite 600
Arlington, VA 22201
Tel: 703-528-1902
http://www.aaanet.org

The AVMA website provides information on student chapters and educational resources.
American Veterinary Medical Association (AVMA)
1931 North Meacham Road, Suite 100
Schaumburg, IL 60173
Tel: 847-925-8070
Email: avmainfo@avma.org
http://www.avma.org

For information on careers in zoos and aquariums, contact
American Zoo and Aquarium Association
8403 Colesville Road, Suite 710
Silver Spring, MD 20910-3314
Tel: 301-562-0777
Email: generalinquiry@aza.org
http://www.aza.org

For information on botany careers, contact
Botanical Society of America
PO Box 299
St. Louis, MO 63166-0299
Tel: 314-577-9566
Email: bsa-manager@botany.org
http://www.botany.org

The LSA website provides descriptions of the various areas of linguistics and a directory of linguistics programs.
Linguistic Society of America (LSA)
1325 18th Street, NW, Suite 211
Washington, DC 20036-6501
Tel: 202-835-1714
Email: lsa@lsadc.org
http://www.lsadc.org

The SAA website lists archaeology programs and features career resources.
Society for American Archaeology (SAA)
900 Second Street, NE, #12
Washington, DC 20002-3560
Tel: 202-789-8200
Email: headquarters@saa.org
http://www.saa.org

This society offers student membership and presents its newsletter online.
Society for Economic Botany
PO Box 1897
Lawrence, KS 66044
Tel: 800-627-0629
http://www.econbot.org

This website features descriptions of and links to ethnomusicology degree programs.
Society for Ethnomusicology
1165 East 3rd Street
Morrison Hall 005
Indiana University
Bloomington, IN 47405-3700
Tel: 812-855-8779
Email: sem@indiana.edu
http://www.ethnomusicology.org

This society offers student memberships.
Society of Ethnobiology
Department of Anthropology
CB 3115, Alumni Building
University of North Carolina-Chapel Hill
Chapel Hill, NC 27599-3155
Email: scarry@email.unc.edu
http://ethnobiology.org

For background information on the field of ethnohistory along with links to schools offering ethnohistory courses, see
American Society for Ethnohistory
http://ethnohistory.org

For materials specifically dealing with ethnoveterinary medicine, see
Ethnovetweb
http://www.ethnovetweb.com

ISE offers a useful list of links to other websites of interest.
International Society for Ethnopharmacology (ISE)
http://www.etnobotanica.de

Food Technologists

OVERVIEW

Food technologists, sometimes known as *food scientists,* study the physical, chemical, and biological composition of food. They develop methods for safely processing, preserving, and packaging food and search for ways to improve its flavor and nutritional value. They also conduct tests to ensure that products, from fresh produce to packaged meals, meet industry and government standards.

HISTORY

One of the earliest methods of food preservation was drying. Grains were sun- and air-dried to prevent mold growth and insect damage. Fruits and vegetables dried in the sun and meats dried and smoked over a fire were stored for use during times of need. Fruits were preserved by fermenting them into wines and vinegars, and fermented milk became curds, cheeses, and yogurts.

Methods of food preservation improved over the centuries, but there were severe limitations until the evolution of scientific methods made it possible to preserve food. By creating conditions unfavorable to the growth or survival of spoilage microorganisms and preventing deterioration by enzymes, scientists were able to extend the storage life of foods well beyond the normal period.

For most of history, people bought or traded for bulk foods, such as grain or rice, rather than prepared foods. This began to change in the early 1800s, when new methods of preserving and packaging foods were developed. The science of food technology did not, however, really develop until shortly before the American entrance into

School Subjects
Chemistry
Mathematics

Personal Skills
Following instructions
Technical/scientific

Work Environment
Primarily indoors
Primarily one location

Minimum Education Level
Bachelor's degree

Salary Range
$29,250 to $49,610 to $86,930

Certification or Licensing
Voluntary

Outlook
About as fast as the average

DOT
311

GOE
02.03.04

NOC
N/A

O*NET-SOC
19-1012.00, 19-4011.02

World War II. Prompted by the need to supply U.S. troops with nutritious, flavorful foods that were not only easy to transport but also kept for long periods of time, scientists around 1940 began making great advances in the preparation, preservation, and packaging of foods. By the 1950s, food science and food technology departments were being established by many universities, and food science disciplines became important and respected areas of study.

Another boost to the food technology program came with the U.S. space program; new types of foods, as well as new types of preparation, packaging, and processing, were needed to feed astronauts in space.

By the late 20th century, few people still canned or preserved their own fruits and vegetables. Advances in production methods in this century have made it possible to process larger quantities of a wider range of food products. Scientists specializing in food technology have found better ways to retard spoilage, improve flavor, and provide foods that are consistent in quality, flavor, texture, and size. Innovations such as freeze drying, irradiation, and artificial coloring and flavoring have changed the way many of the foods we eat are processed and prepared. Consumer demand for an ever-increasing variety of foods has created a demand for food technologists to develop them. Foods processed in a variety of ways are readily available to the consumer and have become such an accepted part of modern life that one rarely gives a thought to the complexities involved. The safety of the process, nutrition, development of new products and production methods, and the packaging of products are all the responsibility of food technologists.

THE JOB

Food technologists usually specialize in one phase of food technology. About one-third are involved in research and development. A large number are employed in quality-control laboratories or in the production or processing areas of food plants. Others teach or perform basic research in colleges and universities, work in sales or management positions, or are employed as technical writers or consultants. The branches of food technology are numerous and include cereal grains, meat and poultry, fats and oils, seafood, animal foods, beverages, dairy products, flavors, sugar and starches, stabilizers, preservatives, colors, and nutritional additives.

Food technologists in basic research study the structure and composition of food and observe the changes that take place during storage or processing. The knowledge they gain may enable them to develop new sources of proteins, determine the effects of processing on microorganisms, or isolate factors that affect the flavor, appearance, or texture of foods. Technologists engaged in applied research and development have the more practical task of creating new food products and developing new processing methods. They also continue to work with existing foods to make them more nutritious and flavorful and to improve their color and texture.

A rapidly growing area of food technology is biotechnology. Food technologists in this area work with plant breeding, gene splicing, microbial fermentation, and plant cell tissue cultures to produce enhanced raw products for processing.

Foods may lose their characteristics (shape, color, etc.) and nutrients during processing and storage. Food technologists seek ways to prevent this by developing improved methods for processing, production, quality control, packaging, and distribution. They conduct chemical and microbiological tests on products to be sure they conform to standards set by the government and by the food industry. They also determine the nutritive content (the amounts of sugar, starch, protein, fat, vitamins, and minerals) that federal regulations say must be printed on the labels.

Food technologists in quality-control laboratories concentrate on ensuring that foods in every stage of processing meet industry and government standards. They check to see that raw ingredients are fresh, sufficiently ripe, and suitable for processing. They conduct periodic inspections of processing line operations. They also test after processing to be sure that various enzymes are not active and that bacteria levels are low enough so the food will not spoil or be unsafe to eat.

Some technologists test new products in test kitchens or develop new processing methods in laboratory pilot plants. Others devise new methods for packaging and storing foods. To solve problems, they may confer with processing engineers, flavor experts, or packaging and marketing specialists.

In processing plants, food technologists are responsible for preparing production specifications and scheduling processing operations. They ensure that proper temperature and humidity levels are maintained in storage areas and that wastes are disposed of properly and other sanitary regulations are observed throughout the plant. They also make recommendations to management in matters relating to efficiency or economy, such as new equipment or suppliers.

Some food technologists have positions in other fields where they can apply their specialized knowledge to such areas as advertising, market research, or technical sales.

Learn More about It

Barham, Peter. *The Science of Cooking.* New York: Springer Verlag, 2001.

Brown, Amy. *Understanding Food: Principles and Preparation.* Stamford, Conn.: Wadsworth Publishing, 1999.

Fellows, P.J. *Food Processing Technology: Principles and Practice.* 2nd ed. Boca Raton, Fla.: CRC Press, 2000.

Jay, James M. *Modern Food Microbiology.* 6th ed. New York: Kluwer Academic/Plenum Publishers, 2000.

Marriott, Norman G. *Principles of Food Sanitation.* 4th ed. New York: Kluwer Academic/Plenum Publishers, 1999.

McSwane, David, et al. *Essentials of Food Safety.* 2d ed. Upper Saddle River, N.J.: Prentice Hall, 2000.

Mizer, David A., ed. *Food Preparation for the Professional.* 3d ed. New York: John Wiley & Sons, 1999.

National Restaurant Association Educational Foundation. *Servsafe Coursebook.* New York: John Wiley & Sons, 2001.

Schlosser, Eric. *Fast Food Nation: The Dark Side of the All-American Meal.* New York: HarperCollins, 2002.

REQUIREMENTS

High School

You can prepare for a technologist career by taking plenty of high school science courses. Be sure to take biology, chemistry, and physics. To get hands-on experience working with food, take family and consumer science classes. Four years of mathematics classes, English classes, computer science classes, and other college-preparatory courses are also important to take.

Postsecondary Training

Educational requirements for this field are high. Beginners need at least a bachelor's degree in food technology, food science, or food engineering. Some technologists hold degrees in other areas, such as chemistry, biology, engineering, agriculture, or business, and nearly half have advanced degrees. Master's degrees and doctorates are mandatory for college teaching and are usually necessary for management and research positions.

Approximately 60 schools offer the course work needed to become a food technologist, and many of these programs have been approved by the Institute of Food Technologists. See the Institute's website (http://www.ift.org) for information on approved schools. Typical courses include physics, biochemistry, mathematics, microbiology, social sciences and humanities, and business administration as well as food technology courses including food preservation, processing, sanitation, and marketing. Most of these schools also offer advanced degrees, usually in specialized areas of food technology. To successfully complete their program, candidates for a master's degree or a doctoral degree must perform extensive research and write a thesis reporting their original findings. Specialists in administrative, managerial, or regulatory areas may earn advanced degrees in business administration or in law rather than in food technology.

Other Requirements

Food technologists should have analytical minds and enjoy technical work. In addition, they must be able to express themselves clearly and be detail oriented. They also must be able to work well in group situations and participate and contribute to a team effort.

EXPLORING

Students may be able to arrange field trips to local food processing plants and plan interviews with or lectures by experts in the field. Apart from an interest in science, and especially chemistry, prospective food technologists may also develop interests in cooking and in inventing their own recipes.

Because of the educational requirements for food technologists, it is not likely that students will be able to acquire actual experience while still in high school. Part-time and summer employment as workers in food processing plants, however, would provide an excellent overview of the industry. More advanced college students may have opportunities for jobs helping out in research laboratories.

EMPLOYERS

Food technologists work in a wide variety of settings, including food processing plants, food ingredient plants, and food manufacturing

Food technologist Alley Watada (left) and horticulturist Ling Qi, who is visiting from China, prepare shredded carrots and other fresh-cut produce for automated measurement of respiration rate and ethylene production. *(Photo by Scott Bauer/USDA)*

plants. They may work in basic research, product development, processing and quality assurance, packaging, or market research. There are positions in laboratories, test kitchens, and on production lines as well as with government agencies.

STARTING OUT

Many schools offering degree programs in food science will also offer job placement assistance. Also, recruiters from private industry frequently conduct interviews on campus. Faculty members may be willing to grant referrals to exceptional students. Another method is to make direct application to individual companies.

Frequently, the food products with which food technologists work determine where they are employed. Those who work with meats or grains may work in the Midwest. Technologists who work with citrus fruits usually work in Florida or California. Two-thirds of all food technologists are employed by private industry. The rest work for the federal government. Some major government employers of food technologists include the Environmental Protection Agency, National Aeronautics and Space Administration, the Food and Drug Administration, and the United States Department of Agriculture.

ADVANCEMENT

For food technologists with a bachelor's degree, there are two general paths to advancement, depending on whether they work in production or in research. They may begin as quality-assurance chemists or assistant production managers and, with experience, move up to more responsible management positions. Some technologists may start as junior food chemists in the research and development laboratory of a food company and advance to section head or another research management position.

Technologists who hold master's degrees may start out as food chemists in a research and development laboratory. Those with doctorates usually begin their careers in basic research or teaching. Other food technologists may gain expertise in more specialized areas and become sensory evaluation experts or food-marketing specialists.

EARNINGS

Salaries for food technologists range from $20,000 to $200,000. According to the *Occupational Outlook Handbook,* median annual earnings of agricultural and food scientists were $49,610 in 2003. The highest paid agricultural and food scientists earned more than $86,930, and the lowest paid earned less than $29,250.

The Institute of Food Technologists reports that their members earned a median salary of $73,150 in 2003. IFT members with a bachelor's degree in food science earned a median salary of $65,000. Members with a master's degree earned a median of $73,500, those with a Ph.D. earned a median of $85,000, and those with an M.B.A. degree earned a median of $95,000 a year.

Most food technologists will receive generous benefit plans, which usually include health insurance, life insurance, pension plans, and vacation and sick pay. Others may receive funds for continuing education.

WORK ENVIRONMENT

Most food technologists work regular hours in clean, well-lighted, temperature-controlled offices, laboratories, or classrooms. Technologists in production and quality-control who work in processing plants may be subject to machine noise and hot or cold conditions.

OUTLOOK

The food industry is the largest single industry in the United States and throughout the world. Because people have to eat, there will always be a need for people to develop, test, and process food products. In developed countries, the ever-present consumer demand for new and different food products means that food scientists and technologists will always be in demand.

Several factors have also created continuing demand for skilled technologists. New labeling laws enacted in the 1990s have required companies to provide detailed nutritional information on their products. The continuing trend toward more healthful eating habits has recently focused on the roles of fats, cholesterol, and salt in nutrition, and companies have rushed to create a variety of low-fat, low-sodium, fat-free, cholesterol-free, and sodium-free foods. A larger and more varied supply of wholesome and economical food is needed to satisfy current tastes. The food industry will have to produce convenience foods of greater quality for use in homes and for the food service institutions that supply airlines, restaurants, and other major customers. More technologists may be hired to research and produce new foods from modifications of wheat, corn, rice, and soybeans, such as the "meat" products made from vegetable proteins. The food industry has increased its spending in recent years for this kind of research and development and is likely to continue to do so. Developing these products, without sacrificing such important factors as taste, appearance, and texture, has produced many new opportunities for food technologists.

Food technologists will also be sought to produce new foods for poor and starving people in underdeveloped countries. Experienced technologists will use their advanced training to create new foods from such staples as rice, corn, wheat, and soybeans.

Finally, the increasing emphasis on the automation of many elements of food processing has also created a need for food technologists to adapt cooking and preparation processes to the new technology.

FOR MORE INFORMATION

For information on accredited food science programs, to read Introduction to the Food Industry, *and to order the booklet* Finding Your First Job in Food Science, *visit the Continuing Education & Professional Development and Employment sections of the IFT website.*

Institute of Food Technologists (IFT)
525 West Van Buren, Suite 1000
Chicago, IL 60607
Tel: 312-782-8424
Email: info@ift.org
http://www.ift.org

For consumer fact sheets, information on issues in the food science industry, and food safety news, visit the NFPA website or contact
National Food Processors Association (NFPA)
1350 I Street, NW, Suite 300
Washington, DC 20005
Tel: 202-639-5900
Email: nfpa@nfpa-food.org
http://www.nfpa-food.org

For national news on agriculture and food issues, contact
U.S. Department of Agriculture
14th Street and Independence Avenue, SW
Washington, DC 20250
http://www.usda.gov

Forensic Experts

OVERVIEW

Forensic experts apply scientific principles and methods to the analysis, identification, and classification of physical evidence relating to criminal (or suspected criminal) cases. They do much of their work in laboratories, where they subject evidence to tests and then record the results. They may travel to crime scenes to collect evidence and record the physical facts of a site. Forensic experts may also be called upon to testify as expert witnesses and to present scientific findings in court.

HISTORY

In Scotland during the late 1780s, a man was convicted of murder when the soles of his boots matched a plaster cast of footprints taken from the scene of the crime. This is one of the earliest recorded cases of the use of physical evidence to link a suspected criminal with the crime.

In the late 19th century, scientists learned to analyze and classify poisons so their presence could be traced in a body. At about the same time, a controversy arose over the different methods being used to identify individuals positively. Fingerprinting emerged in the early 20th century as the most reliable method of personal identification. With the advent of X-ray technology, experts could rely on dental records to substitute for fingerprint analysis when a corpse was in advanced stages of decomposition and the condition of the skin had deteriorated.

Forensic pathology (medical examination of suspicious or unexplained deaths) also came into prominence at this time, as did ballistics, which is the study of projectiles and how they are shot from firearms. The study of ballistics was aided by the invention of the comparison microscope, which enabled an investigator to look at bullets side by side and compare their individual markings. Since individual gun barrels "scar" bullets in a unique pattern, similar markings found on different bullets may prove that they were fired from the same weapon.

These investigations by pioneer forensic scientists led the courts and the police to acknowledge the value of scientifically examined physical evidence in establishing guilt or innocence, confirming identity, proving authenticity of documents, and establishing cause of death. As the result of this acceptance by the legal and law enforcement communities, crime laboratories were established. One of the first, largest, and most complete laboratories is that of the Federal Bureau of Investigation (FBI), founded in 1932. Today, the FBI laboratory examines many thousands of pieces of evidence each year, and its employees present their findings in trials all over the United States and around the world. As the forensic sciences proved their worth, crime laboratories were established in larger cities and by state police departments. These laboratories are used in turn by many communities too small to support labs of their own. The scientific analysis of evidence has become an accepted part of police procedure, and new forensic advances, such as DNA testing, are being developed every day.

THE JOB

Forensic experts, also called *criminalists,* use the instruments of science and engineering to examine physical evidence. They use spectroscopes, microscopes, gas chromatographs, infrared and ultraviolet light, microphotography, and other lab measuring and testing equipment to analyze fibers, fabric, dust, soils, paint chips, glass fragments, fire accelerants, paper and ink, and other substances in order to identify their composition and origin. They analyze poisons, drugs, and other substances found in bodies by examining tissue samples, stomach contents, and blood samples. They analyze and classify blood, blood alcohol, semen, hair, fingernails, teeth, human and animal bones and tissue, and other biological specimens. Using samples of the DNA in these materials, they can match a person with a sample of body tissue. They study documents to determine whether they are forged or genuine. They also examine the physical properties of firearms, bullets, and explosives.

At the scene of a crime (whether actual or suspected), forensic experts collect and label evidence. This painstaking task may involve searching for spent bullets or bits of an exploded bomb and other objects scattered by an explosion. They might look for footprints, fingerprints, and tire tracks, which must be recorded or preserved by plaster casting before they are wiped out. Since crime scenes must eventually be cleaned up, forensic experts take notes and photographs to preserve the arrangement of objects, bodies, and debris. They are sometimes called on later to reconstruct the scene of a crime by making a floor plan or map pinpointing the exact location of bodies, weapons, and furniture.

One important discipline within forensic science is identification. *Fingerprint classifiers* catalog and compare fingerprints of suspected criminals with records to determine if the people who left the fingerprints at the scene of a crime were involved in previous crimes. They often try to match the fingerprints of unknown corpses with fingerprint records to establish their identities. They work in laboratories and offices and travel to other areas such as crime scenes. Retrieving fingerprints outside may be difficult and require specialized processes, such as dusting glassware, windows, or walls with a fine powder. This powder contrasts with many different surfaces and will highlight any fingerprints that remain. Another method of retrieving fingerprints is to lift them off with a flexible tape, which can be brought back to the laboratory for further evaluation and matching.

Fingerprint classifiers compare new prints against those found after the commission of similar crimes. The classifier documents this information and transfers it to the main record-keeping system, often a large mainframe computer system. In the last decade or so, computers have greatly enhanced the possibility of matching new fingerprints to those already on file. A fingerprint classifier may keep individual files on current crimes and note any similarities between them.

Identification technicians work at various jobs related to maintaining police records. In addition to handling fingerprint records, they also work with other kinds of records, such as police reports and eyewitness information about crimes and accidents. They operate equipment used to microfilm police records, as well as store the microfilm and retrieve or copy records upon the request of police or other public officials. *Forensic pathologists* perform autopsies to determine the cause of death; autopsies are almost always performed on victims of crime. *Forensic psychiatrists* also conduct psychiatric evaluations of accused criminals and are often called to testify on whether the accused is mentally fit to stand trial.

Molecular biologists and *geneticists* analyze and review forensic and paternity samples, provide expert testimony in civil and criminal trials, and identify and develop new technologies for use in human identification.

Other job titles within forensic science include *forensic toxicologists,* who are concerned with detecting and identifying the presence of poisons or drugs in a victim's body; *forensic odontologists,* who use dental records and evidence to identify crime victims and to investigate bite marks; and *forensic anthropologists,* who examine and identify bones and skeletal remains.

Forensic experts spend the bulk of their time in the laboratory working with physical evidence. They seldom have direct contact with persons involved in actual or suspected crimes or with police investigators except when collecting evidence and reporting findings. Forensic experts do not interpret their findings relative to the criminal investigation in which they are involved; that is the work of police investigators. The purpose of crime lab work is to provide reliable scientific analysis of evidence that can then be used in criminal investigations and, if needed later, in court proceedings.

REQUIREMENTS

High School
Almost all jobs in this field require at least a bachelor's degree. In high school, you can begin to prepare for a career in forensics by taking a heavy concentration of science courses, including chemistry, biology, physiology, and physics. Computer skills are also important, especially for fingerprint classifiers. A basic grounding in spoken and written communications will be useful because forensic experts must write very detailed reports and are sometimes called on to present their findings in court.

Postsecondary Training
A number of universities and community colleges in the United States offer programs in forensic science, pathology, and various aspects of crime lab work. These courses are often spread throughout the school, in the anatomy, physiology, chemistry, or biology departments, or they may be grouped together as part of the criminal justice department.

Certification or Licensing
Certification may be an advantage for people working in toxicology and document examination. Specialists in these and other disciplines may also be required to take undergraduate and graduate course

Computer-Aided Ballistics Identification

Spent bullets and cartridges, like fingerprints, are unique, each imprinted with striations, or markings, traceable to a single source. For this reason they are often the most telling pieces of evidence found at a crime scene; they are also the most complicated. In the past it often took weeks if not months of comparative microscopic analysis before a firearms expert could link bullets and cartridges to their weapons of origin. Today this process can take less than a day. Technological advances—in computers, networks, imaging devices, and microscopes, among other things—made possible the development of computer-aided ballistics identification. Today this system, accessible to law enforcement agencies around the country, is known as the National Integrated Ballistic Information Network (NIBIN).

In 1992 the Federal Bureau of Investigation (FBI) implemented Drugfire, a computerized system that identified and stored information on gun cartridge cases that were recovered from crime scenes or from test fires of confiscated weapons. When a new casing was brought in for analysis, a firearms examiner added the casing's information to the Drugfire system by placing it on a microscope attached to a computer, which made a computerized image of the casing's breech face marks and firing pin impressions. The image information was committed to the system's databases, and the examiner then had the computer search for images of casings with similar markings already stored in the database. The computer then produced a short list of possible matches for the firearms expert to examine in detail. This process greatly reduced the time it took for examiners to analyze information by hand and determine matches. It also allowed firearms examiners to easily track a weapon and provide law enforcement personnel with information on where and when that weapon had been used before.

work in their areas. In a field such as toxicology, advanced chemistry work is important. The certificate programs are available through the Forensic Sciences Foundation, a branch of the American Academy of Forensic Sciences.

Other Requirements

To be successful in this field, you should have an aptitude for scientific investigation, an inquiring and logical mind, and the ability to make precise measurements and observations. Patience and persistence are important qualities, as is a good memory. Forensic experts must constantly bear in mind that the accuracy of their lab investigations can have great consequences for others.

At about the same time, the Bureau of Alcohol, Tobacco, and Firearms (ATF) began exploring the possibility of using computers, networks, and other technologies to create a database of information on projectiles and cartridge casings from crime guns. To do this, the ATF began using the Integrated Ballistics Identification System (IBIS) in the mid-1990s. This system functioned in much the same way that Drugfire did, using microscope/computer units, databases, and networking. IBIS, however, was also able to incorporate information on severely damaged bullets as well as intact bullets and cartridge casings for matching purposes.

Although both Drugfire and IBIS proved to be excellent law enforcement tools, the two systems were not "interoperable"—that is, they couldn't share information. To bridge this gap, the FBI and ATF began to review and test new systems that would provide a single network, and the NIBIN was created to meet this need. In 2000, implementation of the NIBIN program began, with the ATF responsible for the field operations (including the purchasing of equipment and training of users) and the FBI responsible for the communications network.

Like the two previous systems, NIBIN does not make a positive match of bullets or casings from the same weapon. The system provides firearms examiners with a list of possible matches that they can compare to the physical evidence.

NIBIN has improved on both of these systems and become a powerful weapon used to solve violent crimes. Today there are more than 300,000 images in the system, and thousands of matches, or "hits," have already occurred.

To read success stories involving NIBIN, visit the ATF website at http://www.atf.treas.gov/nibin.

EXPLORING

A large community police department may have a crime lab of its own whose experts can give you specific information about their work and the preparation that helped them build their careers. Smaller communities often use the lab facilities of a larger city nearby or the state police. A school counselor or a representative of the local police may be able to help you arrange a tour of these labs. Lectures in forensic science given at universities or police conventions may also be open to students. Online services and Internet access may provide entry to forums devoted to forensic science and are good sources of information on the daily and professional experiences of people already active in this field.

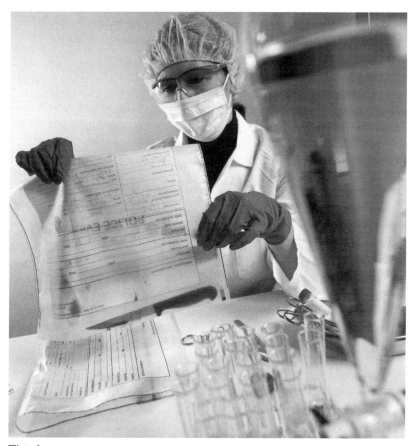

This forensic scientist wears protective gear to prevent contamination while holding an evidence bag containing a knife. Both the knife and the blood found at the crime scene will be analyzed to provide evidence about the crime that has been committed. *(TEK Image / Photo Researchers, Inc.)*

EMPLOYERS

Forensic scientists are typically employed by large police departments or state law enforcement agencies nationwide. However, individuals in certain disciplines are often self-employed or work in the private sector. For example, *forensic engineers,* who use mathematical principles to reconstruct accident scenes, determine the origins of explosions and fires, or review the design of chemical or molecular structures, may be employed by large corporations, small firms, or government agencies. *Forensic anthropologists,* who identify skeletal remains, may work within a university or college, teaching related courses, conducting research, and consulting on cases submitted by law enforcement agencies. They may also be employed by the military or a medical examiner's office. Many forensic science concentrations also offer part-time or consulting opportunities, depending on your level of education and experience.

STARTING OUT

Crime labs are maintained by the federal government and by state and local governments. Applications should be made directly to the personnel department of the government agency supporting the lab. Civil service appointments usually require applicants to take an examination. Such appointments are usually widely advertised well in advance of the application date. Those working for the FBI or other law enforcement agencies usually undergo background checks, which examine their character, background, previous employers, and family and friends.

ADVANCEMENT

In a large crime laboratory, forensic technicians usually advance from an assistant's position to working independently at one or more special types of analysis. From there they may advance to a position as project leader or being in charge of all aspects of one particular investigation. In smaller labs, one technician may have to fill many roles. With experience, such a technician may progress to more responsible work but receive no advancement in title. Fingerprint classifiers who work for police departments may pursue advancement with a different government agency or apply for positions with the FBI.

Crucial to advancement is further education. Forensic experts need to be familiar with scientific procedures such as gas chromatography, ultraviolet and infrared spectrophotometry, mass spectroscopy, electrophoresis, polarizing microscopy, light microscopy, and conventional and isoelectric focusing; knowledge of these analytical techniques and procedures is taught or more fully explored at the master's and doctorate levels. Other, more specific areas of forensics, such as DNA analysis, require advanced degrees in molecular biology and genetics.

EARNINGS

Earnings for forensic analysts vary with the employer, geographic location, and educational and skill levels. Salaries for entry-level

Learn More about It

Baden, Michael, M.D., and Marion Roach. *Dead Reckoning: The New Science of Catching Killers.* New York: Simon & Schuster, 2001.

Camenson, Blythe. *Opportunities in Forensic Science Careers.* New York: McGraw-Hill, 2001.

Evans, Colin. *The Casebook of Forensic Detection: How Science Solved 100 of the World's Most Baffling Crimes.* New York: John Wiley & Sons, 1998.

Fisher, David. *Hard Evidence: How Detectives Inside the FBI's Sci-Crime Lab Have Helped Solve America's Toughest Cases.* New York: Dell Books, 1996.

Kruse, Warren G., II, and Jay G. Heiser. *Computer Forensics: Incident Response Essentials.* Reading, Mass.: Addison-Wesley, 2001.

Nickell, Joe, and John F. Fischer. *Crime Science: Methods of Forensic Detection.* Lexington, Ky.: University Press of Kentucky, 1998.

Ramsland, Katherine M. *The Forensic Science of C.S.I.* New York: Berkley Boulevard, 2001.

Sachs, Jessica Snyder. *Corpse: Nature, Forensics, and the Struggle to Pinpoint Time of Death.* Boulder, Colo.: Perseus Books Group, 2001.

Sullivan, Patrick J., et al. *Practical Environmental Forensics: Process and Case Histories.* New York: John Wiley & Sons, 2000.

Zonderman, Jon. *Beyond the Crime Lab: The New Science of Investigation.* New York: John Wiley & Sons, 1998.

positions as research assistants or technicians working in local and regional labs range from $20,000 to $25,000. For those individuals with a bachelor's degree and two to five years of specialized experience, salaries range from $30,000 to $40,000. Salaries for those with advanced degrees range from $50,000 to well over $100,000 a year. The U.S. Department of Labor reports that the median annual salary for forensic experts was $43,200 in 2003. Salaries ranged from less than $26,520 to more than $70,830 per year.

WORK ENVIRONMENT

Forensic experts usually perform the analytical portion of their work in clean, quiet, air-conditioned laboratories, but they are frequently required to travel to crime scenes to collect evidence or study the site to understand more fully the evidence collected by detectives. When gathering evidence and analyzing it, forensic experts need to be able to concentrate, sometimes in crowded, noisy situations. For this reason, forensic experts must be adaptable and able to work in a variety of environments, including dangerous or unpleasant places.

Many crime scenes are grisly and may be extremely distressing for beginning workers and even for more seasoned professionals. In addition, forensic experts who work with human remains will regularly view corpses, and, more often than not, these corpses will have been mutilated in some way or be in varying degrees of decomposition. Individuals interested in this field need to develop the detachment and objectivity necessary to view corpses and extract specimens for testing and analysis.

Simulating the precise conditions of a crime site for a full analysis is often crucial, so forensic experts often return to the site so that they can perform tests or functions outside of the controlled environment of their lab. When traveling to the scene of a crime, forensic experts may have to carry cases of tools, cameras, and chemicals. In order not to risk contaminating evidence, they must follow strict procedures (both in and out of the laboratory) for collecting and testing evidence; these procedures can be extremely time-consuming and thus require a great deal of patience. Forensic experts also need to be able to arrive at and present their findings impartially. In large labs, they often work as part of a team under the direction of a senior technologist. They may experience eyestrain and contact with strong chemicals, but little heavy physical work is involved.

OUTLOOK

The number of forensic experts employed in the United States is expected to grow about as fast as the average for all other occupations over the next decade, according to the U.S. Department of Labor. This is a small career group, numbering only a few thousand (not including the many scientific experts who are called in as consultants when their expertise is needed). Population increases, a rising crime rate, and the greater emphasis on scientific methodology in crime investigation, however, will likely increase the need for trained experts. Some government agencies may be under pressure to reduce staff because of budget problems.

FOR MORE INFORMATION

For information on certification, careers, and colleges and universities that offer forensic science programs, contact
   American Academy of Forensic Sciences
   PO Box 669
   Colorado Springs, CO 80901-0669
   Tel: 719-636-1100
   http://www.aafs.org

To learn more about forensic services at the FBI, visit the FBI Laboratory Division website.
   Federal Bureau of Investigation (FBI)
   J. Edgar Hoover Building
   935 Pennsylvania Avenue, NW, Room 7972
   Washington, DC 20535
   Tel: 202-324-3000
   http://www.fbi.gov

For additional information on forensics and forensics professionals, contact the following organizations:
   American Society of Questioned Document Examiners
   PO Box 18298
   Long Beach, CA
   Email: jlee@ci.west-valley.ut.us
   http://www.asqde.org

   Society of Forensic Toxicologists
   PO Box 5543
   Mesa, AZ 85211-5543
   Tel: 480-839-9106
   http://www.soft-tox.org

Genetic Scientists

OVERVIEW

Genetic scientists, or *geneticists,* study heredity. They study plants as well as animals, including humans. Geneticists conduct research on how characteristics are passed from one generation to the next through the genes present in each cell of an organism. This research often involves manipulating or altering particular genetic characteristics to better understand how genetic systems work. For instance, genetic scientists may breed a family of mice with a tendency toward high blood pressure to test the effects of exercise or diet on that condition. Their work adds to the body of biological knowledge and helps prevent inheritable diseases. Genetics is a component of just about every area of biology and can be found in many biology subfields. Rapidly growing specialty areas include the fields of genetic counseling and medical genetics, and the role of genetics in medicine.

HISTORY

In the 1860s, an Austrian monk named Gregor Mendel discovered the principles of genetics by breeding different varieties of garden peas in his monastery garden. His experiments, which showed that crossing short and tall peas produced only tall plants rather than any of medium height, proved that no blending of traits occurred. Rather, tallness was the dominant (or more powerful) trait and shortness was recessive.

Fifty years after Mendel's discoveries, American biologist Thomas Hunt Morgan discovered that genes are located on the chromosomes present in every cell. Genes are like a blueprint: They carry instructions for how an organism—human, animal, or plant—will be built.

However, as Hugo de Vries discovered in his research in the early 1900s, genes do not always copy themselves exactly. Sometimes they mutate, that is, change their blueprint from one generation to the next. Mutations are often responsible for illness.

The modern history of genetics began in the early 1950s with James Watson's and Francis Crick's discovery of the double helix, or spiral ladder, structure of DNA. Their discovery touched off a flurry of scientific activity that led to a better understanding of DNA chemistry and the genetic code. Before 1975, however, the technology for actually altering the genes of organisms for study or practical use was severely limited. For while the 1950s and 1960s saw big successes in gene transfer and molecular biology for the smaller and simpler bacteria cells, more complex organisms were another story. Even though both plant and animal cells could be grown in culture, the detailed workings of their genes remained a mystery until the discovery of recombinant DNA techniques. Recombinant DNA refers to combining the DNA, or genetic material, from two separate organisms to form unique DNA molecules that carry a new combination of genes. The major tools of this technology—and the second most important discovery in the field of genetics—are restriction enzymes, first discovered in the 1960s. They work by cutting up DNA molecules at particular points so that DNA pieces from different sources may be joined. These genetically engineered cells may then be cloned, or grown in culture, to make copies of the desired gene. The cloning of genetically engineered cells has many potentially useful applications for society, such as producing pest-resistant plants, altering bacteria for waste cleanup, or generating proteins for medical uses like dissolving blood clots or making human growth hormone.

The most ambitious project in DNA research to date made possible by advanced technology was the effort to map the entire human genome, or all the genetic material in human beings. Called the Human Genome Project (HGP), it is considered more important to science history than either the splitting of the atom or the moon landing. The U.S. government launched the HGP in 1990, with the goal of completing the sequencing by 2005. In 1998, Celera Genomics Corporation (a for-profit company) announced that it would start its own sequencing project to compete with the HGP. By 2000 (four years ahead of schedule), both organizations had completed rough drafts of the human genome. Project results promise new scientific knowledge, medicines, and therapies that can be used to battle diseases such as AIDS, cancer, arthritis, and osteoporosis. Continuing advances in automation and electronics, including use of the latest computer software, will greatly promote project goals and increase our understanding of genetics.

THE JOB

The goal of genetic scientists is to increase biological knowledge so as to understand and cure genetic diseases; counsel families at risk of having children with genetic defects; and breed new crops and livestock, among other things. Most geneticists spend their time in a laboratory isolating particular genes in tissue samples and doing experiments to find out which characteristics those genes are responsible for. They work with chemicals, heat, light, and such instruments as microscopes, computers, electron microscopes, and other technical equipment. Besides having excellent mathematical and analytical skills, which will help them design and carry out experiments and analyze results, genetic scientists must also develop good writing and teaching techniques. They must be able to communicate their research results to students in classroom settings and to colleagues through published papers.

Profound academic and technological advances made over the last decade have brought about rapid progress in the field and opened up a whole new world for genetic scientists, who can now go just about anywhere their imagination leads them. Some of the many specialty areas for geneticists are described here.

Research geneticists typically complete a Ph.D. program, carrying out original research under a faculty member's direction. After earning their Ph.D.'s, most graduates do research for two to four years as postdoctoral fellows. Following this training, they are then qualified to hold faculty positions at academic institutions or to join the staffs of research institutes or biotechnology firms.

Laboratory geneticists apply modern genetic technology to agriculture, police work, pharmaceutical development, and clinical medicine. They typically have four to six years of college and are part of a staff of scientists trained in molecular biology, cytogenetics, biochemical genetics, immunogenetics, and related disciplines. Some genetic laboratories require their staff members to have specific training and certification in cytogenetic or medical technology.

Some genetic scientists specialize as *genetic counselors*. They are health professionals with specialized graduate degrees in medical genetics and counseling. They work as a valuable part of a health care team, giving information and support to families with birth defects or genetic disorders. They also help individuals who themselves have genetic conditions and counsel couples concerned about passing a harmful gene to a child. Genetic counselors identify families at risk, take down family medical histories, and obtain and interpret information about genetic conditions. They perform blood tests to detect possible harmful genes and predict the likelihood of genetic diseases occurring in children. Genetic counselors run down available options with their clients, serving as patient advocates and making referrals to community or state support services. Some genetic counselors serve in administrative roles, while many conduct research activities related to the field of medical genetics and genetic counseling.

Clinical geneticists are even more highly trained specialists in the genetics field. They are generally medical doctors, having received an M.D. degree and completed a pediatric, internal medicine, or obstetric residency, followed by specialized genetics training. Many clinical geneticists work at university medical centers or large hospitals, while some have private practices. Generally, this job involves recognizing genetic disorders and birth defects, understanding what they mean for the patient, arranging the proper treatment, and helping the patient and family understand and cope with the disorder. Some clinical geneticists work mainly with infants and children, while others may specialize in the genetic problems of babies still in the womb. They may also work with adult patients with inherited forms of heart disease, cancer, or neurological disease. An increasingly important role for the clinical geneticist is to be the link between scientists who are constantly advancing the field and the patients who stand to benefit from their discoveries.

Cytogenetic technologists study chromosome structure and function. They analyze chromosomes by making them visible under light microscopy. Living cells are first treated with a special stain that reveals stripes of light and dark regions along the length of each chromosome. Because the stripes are highly specific for a particular chromosome, stripe patterns help differentiate chromosomes from one another, making any abnormalities in number easily seen. Chromosome analysis may be done on just about any living tissue, but for clinical work, it usually is done on amniotic fluid (fluid surrounding the fetus), chorionic villi (fetal placenta), blood, bone marrow, and miscarriages. The work is challenging, like piecing together a jigsaw puzzle.

Molecular geneticists study DNA, the blueprint for protein molecules in cells. An offshoot of cytogenetics, forensic genetics, is used by the law enforcement community to perform DNA fingerprinting, a subspecialty that is currently booming. Alec Jeffreys, a professor at Leicester University, discovered that each of us has highly specific pat-

This genetic scientist is mixing reagents in a laboratory. *(Pierre Schwartz/Corbis)*

terns within our DNA located on many different chromosomes. The pattern is so distinctive that no two people's are the same, except for identical twins, which is why the technique is called DNA fingerprinting. It has been used to identify and convict criminals and to determine parentage.

Genetic engineers experiment with altering, splicing, and rearranging genes for specific results. This research has resulted in the discovery and production of insulin and interferon, two medical breakthroughs that can treat genetically caused diseases like diabetes. Agricultural triumphs like hybrid corn, disease-resistant grains, and higher quality livestock are all products of the principles of recombinant DNA and cloning.

Another specialty area for geneticists is population genetics. *Population geneticists* examine the breeding methods of farm animals and crops. They look at mutations that occur spontaneously or are introduced purposely to produce a marketable result.

REQUIREMENTS

High School

If you are interested in becoming a geneticist working in basic research, you should study math, chemistry, and physics in high school, along with biology. English, writing, and computer studies are helpful for developing communications skills. A college degree is a must.

Postsecondary Training

In college, students wishing to become basic research geneticists typically major in biology or genetics, taking math, chemistry, and physics courses as well. However, you could also major in any one of the physical sciences with a minor in biology and still enter graduate school in the field of genetics. At public and private universities, colleges, and medical schools, genetic scientists almost always hold doctoral degrees and teach undergraduate and graduate courses in addition to doing research. Clinical geneticists usually earn an M.D. degree, which requires getting admitted to medical school, then completing a three- to-five-year residency in a medical specialty followed by an additional two to three years of specialized training in genetics.

Career opportunities also exist for those with bachelor's or master's of science degrees, particularly in the rapidly growing biotechnology field, which is using genetics to produce everything from medicines to microchips. This industry needs well-trained research technicians who typically have a bachelor of science degree in biology with a molecular or biochemistry emphasis. The federal government also has a need for research technicians and hires college graduates and those with master's degrees to work in hospitals and U.S. Department of Agriculture (USDA) laboratories. Cytogenetic technologists generally need a bachelor of science degree.

Genetic counselors usually hold specialized graduate degrees. Training programs for genetic counselors are two-year master's-level programs with courses and field training in medical genetics and counseling.

Certification or Licensing

Geneticists do not need to be licensed. However, those with clinical practices in human or medical genetics may get certification through both the American Board of Medical Genetics (http://www.abmg.org) and the American Board of Genetic Counseling (http://www.abgc.net). Some genetic laboratories require staff to have specific training and certification in cytogenetic or medical technology, while others hire people with any relevant B.S. or M.S. degree as long as they show an aptitude for the work. Graduates of a master's degree program in genetic counseling can apply to sit for the certification examination of the American Board of Genetic Counseling.

Other Requirements

Geneticists must be smart and have inquiring minds. They need to be able to evaluate results and draw conclusions from measurable criteria. They should also be able to work with abstract theories and ideas, and in cooperation with others. Both written and verbal communications skills are important for sharing research information. Important personal qualities for laboratory scientists are patience, attention to detail, and determination. Genetic counselors must have mature judgment and strong communications skills to deal with people coping with highly emotional issues. They must be able to establish trust quickly and have the right mix of objectivity (the ability to be neutral) and sensitivity to do their work well.

EXPLORING

As a high school student, you can prepare for a career as a genetic scientist by taking as many courses in math and science as you can. You should also develop your writing and computer skills. High school science teachers can often contact departments of biology and genetics at nearby colleges and universities and arrange field trips or college speakers. Speakers can give you information about university summer programs. Take advantage of these and other opportunities offered in your community through community colleges, museums, professional associations, and special interest groups.

EMPLOYERS

Genetic scientists work for a variety of employers, including biotechnology firms, research centers, government agencies, and agricultural stations and farms. Government laboratories that employ genetic scientists include the USDA, the Fish and Wildlife Service, the National Institutes of Health, and several others. Genetic scientists are also needed by agricultural colleges seeking practical applications of genetics for livestock, poultry, or crops. Genetic scientists working in this setting divide their time between teaching and research programs. Most of these jobs are in college and university departments of biology, botany, zoology, or microbiology.

STARTING OUT

Because this career is so broad with many varied fields within it, methods of entry also vary, depending on the specialty area you choose. As early as high school, opportunities exist for paid and unpaid internships at a number of science laboratories. Job seekers can get leads from their professors or fellow students. You could join a team of researchers as a laboratory aide or technician.

If you are interested in a job with the federal government, contact a local Federal Job Information Office or regional Office of Personnel Management to find out which tests you need to take. Federal agencies also come to college campuses to recruit graduates. You can look up federal job openings in the biweekly *Federal Career Opportunities* bulletin, available by subscription and at your local library, and apply directly to the federal agency or department you are interested in. You can also look up federal job openings online at http://www.fedjobs.com.

If you would like to work at a college or university after completing an advanced degree, you may wish to continue your education through a postdoctoral fellowship, assisting a prominent scientist with research. Colleges and universities advertise open positions in professional journals and in the *Chronicle of Higher Education*, available at public libraries. You should also consult pharmaceutical and biotechnology companies' departments of human resources for employment opportunities in those industries.

ADVANCEMENT

At colleges and universities, beginning teachers and researchers are hired at the assistant professor level. With additional years of experience and an impressive level of published research and teaching, they are promoted to associate professor and then to full professor. Similar years of experience lead to promotion in private industry and government agencies. Promotion usually involves an increase in salary as well as more job duties and greater work prominence.

EARNINGS

The starting salary in 2005 for genetic scientists with a bachelor's degree hired by the federal government at the GS-5 entry level was $24,677. For those with a master's degree, who qualified to start at the GS-7 or GS-9 levels, the beginning salary was $30,567 and $37,390, respectively. Doctoral degree holders who qualified to start at the GS-11 level earned $45,239. The average salary for genetic scientists working in private industry is approximately $55,000, with biotechnology firms offering even higher salaries. The highest paid, most experienced genetic scientists make upwards of $70,000 to $80,000 a year. Universities, which generally hire only geneticists with doctoral degrees, offer starting salaries ranging from $31,000 for new assistant professors to $52,000 for full professors.

According to a member survey by the National Society of Genetic Counselors, genetic counselors earned annual salaries that ranged from $23,871 to $112,000 in 2002. The survey also reported the following 2002 median earnings for genetic counselors by specialty: pediatrics, $45,000; prenatal, $46,538; cancer, $48,325; molecular/cytogenetics/biochemical testing, $45,500; and specialty disease, $48,250.

WORK ENVIRONMENT

Genetic scientists spend most of their time in laboratories, designing and conducting research experiments. Most of these experiments will take many hours and yield few publishable results. But while breakthrough discoveries occur rarely and often involve hours of repetitive work, they can result in patents and significant royalties, not to mention the payoff of lives saved or diseases eliminated. Even small discoveries in the genetics field add to biological knowledge and can often lead to elimination of disease. Genetic scientists also spend considerable time writing reports about their experiments, lecturing or teaching about their research, and preparing grant proposals to federal or private agencies to secure funding to support their research. Because federal grants are extremely competitive, only the best-written and most scientifically up-to-date proposals will receive funding. Therefore, genetic scientists must keep improving their skills and knowledge throughout their careers to keep up with new developments in the field and to advance their own research. Usually, geneticists work as part of a research team, cooperating on various aspects of their experiments. Geneticists often head up teams of researchers, graduate students, and laboratory personnel. They may work from nine to five, although they may be required to work late into the night and on weekends during critical periods of an experiment. They may also work extra hours to complete research projects, to write reports of findings, or to read the latest developments in their specialty. Like other life scientists, geneticists must study throughout their careers to keep up with new developments in the field and to advance their own research.

OUTLOOK

The U.S. Department of Labor predicts about average job growth for the field of biological science through 2012, but opportunities for genetic scientists should be even better. Interest in genetic research has exploded in the past decade, with breakthrough discoveries bringing greater attention to the exciting possibilities of finding genetic causes and cures for diseases.

Working in an age with virtually no limits, geneticists have the luxury of choosing their focus according to what interests them most. Rapid progress in the field, along with new methods of mapping genetic traits, has put all natural variation in all organisms within the grasp of genetic investigators. It is estimated that every human disease that is caused by a single gene defect will be curable by genetic intervention during the lifetime of students currently in high school. As the need to understand human and animal biology and genetics and the fight to eradicate disease continue, demand for scientists will continue to increase. The world of criminal investigation is increasingly using genetics to win cases, drawing on genetic test results to identify culprits from a drop of blood. Genetics is also being used in food testing to detect the slightest contamination by disease-causing organisms.

Genetics clearly stands out as the field of the future. A survey conducted by the American Association for the Advancement of Science in the 1990s asked its 2,500 members to name the scientific specialty with the most promise for the next decade. Genetics was listed as the number one choice by biologists, physicists and astronomers, social and behavioral scientists, and chemists. It was listed as the second most promising field by medical scientists, engineers, and earth scientists.

FOR MORE INFORMATION

For information on certification and a listing of accredited graduate schools, contact
　　American Board of Genetic Counseling
　　9650 Rockville Pike
　　Bethesda, MD 20814-3998
　　Tel: 301-634-7316
　　http://www.abgc.net

For information about medical genetics, contact
　　American Board of Medical Genetics
　　9650 Rockville Pike
　　Bethesda, MD 20814-3998
　　Tel: 301-634-7315
　　http://www.abmg.org

For information on educational programs and career guides, contact
American Society of Human Genetics
9650 Rockville Pike
Bethesda, MD 20814
Tel: 866-486-4363
Email: society@ashg.org
http://www.ashg.org

To read the online publication Careers in Genetics, *visit the GSA website.*
Genetics Society of America (GSA)
9650 Rockville Pike
Bethesda, MD 20814-3998
Tel: 301-634-7300
http://www.genetics-gsa.org

For comprehensive information on genetic counseling as a career, contact or visit the following website:
National Society of Genetic Counselors
233 Canterbury Drive
Wallingford, PA 19086-6617
Tel: 610-872-7608
Email: fyi@nsgc.org
http://www.nsgc.org

Marine Biologists

OVERVIEW

Marine biologists study species of plants and animals living in saltwater, their interactions with one another, and how they influence and are influenced by environmental factors. Marine biology is a branch of the biological sciences, and biologists in this area work in many different industries, including government agencies, universities, aquariums, and fish hatcheries, to name a few. They generally work either in a laboratory setting or in the field, which in this case means being in or on the ocean or its margins.

HISTORY

Marine biologists started to make their study into a real science around the 19th century with a series of British expeditions. In 1872, the HMS *Challenger* set sail with scientists Sir Charles Wyville Thomson and Sir John Murray on the most important oceanographic mission of all time. Over four years, they traveled 69,000 miles and cataloged 4,717 new species of marine plants and animals. Many marine scientists view the reports from this expedition as the basis of modern oceanography.

Before this time, marine scientists believed that sea creatures inhabited only shallow waters. They believed that the intense cold, pressure, and darkness below about 1,800 feet could not support life. Then, in the late 1860s, the HMS *Lightning* and the HMS *Porcupine* made hauls from below 14,400 feet that contained bizarre new creatures.

Scientists began to build precision equipment for measuring oceanic conditions. Among these were thermometers that could gauge the temperature at any depth, containers that could be closed at a desired depth to collect seawater, and coring instruments used to sample bottom sediments. Scientists also figured out techniques for measuring levels of salt, oxygen, and nutrients right on board ship.

Twentieth-century innovations such as underwater cameras, oxygen tanks, submersible craft, and heavy-duty diving gear that can withstand extremes of cold and pressure have made it possible for marine biologists to observe sea creatures in their natural habitats.

THE JOB

Marine biologists study and work with sea creatures in their natural environment, the oceans of the world and tidal pools along shorelines, as well as in laboratories. These scientists are interested in knowing how the ocean's changing conditions, such as temperature and chemical pollutants, can affect the plants and animals that live there. For example, what happens when certain species become extinct or are no longer safe to be eaten? Marine biologists can begin to understand how the world's food supply is diminished and help come up with solutions that can change such problem situations.

The work of these scientists is also important for improving and controlling sport and commercial fishing. Through underwater exploration, marine biologists have discovered that humans are damaging the world's coral reefs. They have also charted the migration of whales and counted the decreasing numbers of certain species. They have observed dolphins being accidentally caught in tuna fishermen's nets. By writing reports and research papers about such discoveries, a marine biologist can inform others about problems that need attention and begin to make important changes that could help the world.

To study plants and animals, marine biologists spend some of their work time in the ocean wearing wetsuits to keep warm (because of the frigid temperature below the surface of the sea) and scuba gear to breathe underwater. They gather specimens with a slurp gun, which sucks fish into a specimen bag without injuring them. They must learn how to conduct their research without damaging the marine environment, which is delicate. Marine biologists must also face the threat to their own safety from dangerous fish and underwater conditions.

Marine biologists also study life in tidal pools along the shoreline. They might collect specimens at the same time of day for days at a time. They would keep samples from different pools separate and keep records of the pool's location and the types and measurements of the specimens taken. This ensures that the studies are as accurate as possible. After collecting specimens, they keep them in a portable aquarium tank on board ship. After returning to land, which may not be for weeks or months, marine biologists study specimens in a laboratory, often with other scientists working on the same study. They might, for example, check the amount of oxygen in a sea turtle's bloodstream to learn how the turtles can stay underwater for so long, or measure elements in the blood of an arctic fish to discover how it can survive frigid temperatures.

REQUIREMENTS

High School

If you are interested in this career, begin your preparations by taking plenty of high school science classes, such as biology, chemistry, and earth science. Also take math classes and computer science classes, both of which will give you skills that you will use in doing research. In addition, take English classes, which will also help you develop research skills as well as writing skills. And, because you will probably need to extend your education beyond the level of a bachelor's degree, consider taking a foreign language. Many graduate programs require their students to meet a foreign language requirement.

Postsecondary Training

In college, take basic science courses such as biology, botany, and chemistry. However, your class choices don't end there. For instance, in biology you might be required to choose from marine invertebrate biology, ecology, oceanography, genetics, animal physiology, plant physiology, and aquatic plant biology. You might also be required to choose several more specific classes from such choices as ichthyology, vertebrate structure, population biology, developmental biology, biology of microorganisms, evolution, and cell biology. Classes in other subjects will also be required, such as computer science, math (including algebra, trigonometry, calculus, analytical geometry, and statistics), and physics.

Although it is possible to get a job as a marine biologist with just a bachelor's degree, such jobs likely will be low-paying technician positions with little advancement opportunities. Most marine biologists have a master's or doctoral degree. The American Society of Limnology and Oceanography website (http://www.aslo.org) has links to programs offering graduate degrees in aquatic science. Students at the graduate level begin to develop an area of specialization, such as aquatic chemical ecology (the study of chemicals and their effect on aquatic environments) and bioinformatics (the use of computer science, math, and statistics to analyze genetic information). Master's degree programs generally take two to three years to complete. Programs leading to a Ph.D. typically take four to five years to complete.

Certification or Licensing

If you are going to be diving, organizations like the Professional Association of Diving Instructors provide basic certification. Training for scientific diving is more in-depth and requires passing an exam. It is also critical that divers learn cardiopulmonary resuscitation (CPR) and first aid. Also, if you'll be handling hazardous materials such as formaldehyde, strong acids, or radioactive nucleotides, you must be licensed.

Other Requirements

You should have an ability to ask questions and solve problems, observe small details carefully, do research, and analyze mathematical information. You should be inquisitive and must be able to think for yourself. This is essential to the scientific method. You must use your creative ability and be inventive in order to design experiments; these are the scientist's means of asking questions of the natural world. Working in the field often requires some strength and physical endurance, particularly if you are scuba diving or if you are doing fieldwork in tidepools, which can involve hiking over miles of shore at low tide, keeping your footing on weedy rocks, and lifting and turning stones to find specimens.

EXPLORING

Explore this career and your interest in it by joining your high school's science club. If the club is involved in any type of projects or experiments, you will have the opportunity to begin learning to work with others on a team as well as develop your science and lab skills. If you are lucky enough to live in a city with an aquarium, be sure to get either paid or volunteer work there. This is an excellent way to learn about marine life and about the life of a marine biologist. Visit Sea Grant's marine careers website (http://www.marinecareers.net) for links to information on internships, volunteerships, and other activities, such as sea camps.

You can begin diving training while you are in high school. If you are between the ages of 10 and 14, you can earn a junior open water diver certification. When you turn 15 you can upgrade your certification to open water diver.

Aquariums on the Web

Alaska SeaLife Center
http://www.alaskasealife.org

Aquarium of the Bay
http://www.aquariumofthebay.com

Gulf of Maine Research Institute
http://www.gma.org

John G. Shedd Aquarium
http://www.sheddnet.org

Miami Seaquarium
http://www.miamiseaquarium.com

National Aquarium in Baltimore
http://aqua.org

Oregon Coast Aquarium
http://www.aquarium.org

Seattle Aquarium
http://www.seattleaquarium.org

Waikiki Aquarium
http://waquarium.otted.hawaii.edu

EMPLOYERS

Employers in this field range from pharmaceutical companies researching marine sources for medicines to federal agencies that regulate marine fisheries, such as the fisheries division of the National Oceanographic and Atmospheric Administration. Aquariums hire marine biologists to collect and study specimens.

After acquiring many years of experience, marine biologists with Ph.D.'s may be eligible for faculty positions at a school like the Scripps Institute of Oceanography or the University of Washington.

Marine products companies that manufacture carrageenan and agar (extracted from algae and used as thickening agents in foods) hire marine biologists to design and carry out research.

Jobs in marine biology are based mostly in coastal areas, though some biologists work inland as university professors or perhaps as paleontologists who search for and study marine fossils.

STARTING OUT

With a bachelor's degree only, you may be able to get a job as a laboratory technician in a state or federal agency. Some aquaria will hire you straight out of college, but generally it's easier to get a paid position if you've worked as a volunteer at an aquarium. You'll need a more advanced degree to get into more technical positions such as consulting, writing for scientific journals, and conducting research.

Websites are good resources for employment information. If you can find the human resources section of an aquarium's home page, it will tell you whom to contact to find out about openings and may even provide job listings. Federal agencies may also have websites with human resource information.

Professors who know you as a student might be able to help you locate a position through their contacts in the professional world.

Another good way to make contacts is by attending conferences or seminars sponsored by aquatic science organizations such as the American Society of Limnology and Oceanography or the Mid-Atlantic Marine Education Association.

ADVANCEMENT

Lab technicians with four-year degrees may advance to become senior lab techs after years with the same lab. Generally, though, taking on greater responsibility or getting into more technical work means having more education. Those wanting to do research (in any setting) will need a graduate degree or at least to be working on one. To get an administrative position with a marine products company or a faculty position at a university, marine biologists need at least a master's degree, and those wanting to become senior scientists at a marine station or full professors must have a doctoral degree.

EARNINGS

Salaries vary quite a lot depending on factors such as the person's level of education, the type of work (research, teaching, etc.), the size, location, and type of employer (for example, large university, government agency, or private company), and the person's level of work experience. According to the National Association of Colleges and

This marine biology student is examining a starfish in a laboratory. *(Brownie Harris/Corbis)*

Employers' *Salary Survey* of September 2003, those seeking their first job and holding bachelor's degrees in biological sciences had average salary offers of $29,456. The American Society of Limnology and Oceanography reports that those with bachelor's degrees may start out working for federal government agencies at the pay grades GS-5 to GS-7. In 2005 the yearly earnings at the GS-5 level ranged from $24,677 to $32,084, and yearly earnings at the GS-7 level ranged from $30,567 to $39,738. Income for marine biologists who hold full-time positions at colleges and universities will be similar to those of other full-time faculty. The American Association of University Professors' *Annual Report on the Economic Status of the Profession 2003–2004* found that college teachers (regardless of their subject area) averaged a yearly income of approximately $66,475. It also reports that professors averaged the following salaries by rank: full professors, $88,591; associate professors, $63,063; assistant professors, $52,788; and instructors, $38,501. Marine biologists who hold top-ranking positions and have much experience, such as senior research scientists, may make more than these amounts.

Benefits vary by employer but often include such extras as health insurance and retirement plans.

WORK ENVIRONMENT

Most marine biologists don't actually spend a lot of time diving. However, researchers might spend a couple of hours periodically breathing from a scuba tank below some waters, like Monterey Bay or the Gulf of Maine. They might gather samples from the deck of a large research vessel during a two-month expedition, or they might meet with several other research biologists.

In most marine biology work, some portion of time is spent in the lab, analyzing samples of seawater or collating data on a computer. Many hours are spent in solitude, reading papers in scientific journals or writing papers for publication.

Instructors or professors work in classrooms interacting with students and directing student lab work.

Those who work for an aquarium, as consultants for private corporations, or in universities work an average of 40 to 50 hours a week.

OUTLOOK

Generally speaking, there are more marine biologists than there are paying positions at present. Changes in the Earth's environment, such as global warming and increased levels of heavy metals in the global water cycle, will most likely prompt more research and result in slightly more jobs in different subfields.

Greater need for smart management of the world's fisheries, research by pharmaceutical companies into deriving medicines from marine organisms, and cultivation of marine food alternatives such as seaweeds and plankton are other factors that may increase the demand for marine biologists in the near future. Because of strong competition for jobs, however, employment should grow about as fast as the average.

FOR MORE INFORMATION

The education and outreach section of AIBS's website has information on a number of careers in biology.
American Institute of Biological Sciences (AIBS)
1444 Eye Street, NW, Suite 200

Washington, DC 20005
Tel: 202-628-1500
http://www.aibs.org

Visit ASLO's website for information on careers and education. For information on membership and publications, contact
American Society of Limnology and Oceanography (ASLO)
5400 Bosque Boulevard, Suite 680
Waco, TX 76710
Tel: 800-929-2756
Email: business@aslo.org
http://www.aslo.org

For information on volunteer programs for in-state students and college internships, contact
National Aquarium in Baltimore
Conservation Education Department-Internships
501 East Pratt Street
Baltimore, MD 21202
Tel: 410-576-3800
http://aqua.org

For information on diving instruction and certification, contact PADI.
Professional Association of Diving Instructors (PADI)
30151 Tomas Street
Rancho Santa Margarita, CA 92688-2125
Tel: 800-729-7234
http://www.padi.com

This center for research and education in global science currently runs more than 300 research programs and uses a fleet of four ships to conduct expeditions over the entire globe. For more information, contact
Scripps Institution of Oceanography
University of California-San Diego
8602 La Jolla Shores Drive
La Jolla, CA 92037
http://www.sio.ucsd.edu

For reference lists, links to marine labs, summer intern and course opportunities, and links to career information, check out the following website

Marine Biology Web

http://life.bio.sunysb.edu/marinebio/mbweb.html

For links to career information and sea programs, visit the following websites:

Careers in Oceanography, Marine Science, and Marine Biology

http://scilib.ucsd.edu/sio/guide/career.html

Sea Grant's Marinecareers.net

http://www.marinecareers.net

Naturalists

QUICK FACTS

School Subjects
Biology
Earth science
English

Personal Skills
Communication/ideas
Technical/scientific

Work Environment
Primarily outdoors
One location with some
  travel

Minimum Education Level
Bachelor's degree

Salary Range
$24,677 to $50,340 to
  $74,025+

Certification or Licensing
None available

Outlook
Little change or more slowly
  than the average

DOT
049

GOE
12.01.01

NOC
2121

O*NET-SOC
19-1031.03

OVERVIEW

The primary role of *naturalists* is to educate the public about the environment and maintain the natural environment on land specifically dedicated to wilderness populations. Their primary responsibilities are preserving, restoring, maintaining, and protecting a natural habitat. Among the related responsibilities in these jobs are teaching, public speaking, writing, giving scientific and ecological demonstrations, and handling public relations and administrative tasks. Naturalists may work in a variety of environments, including private nature centers; local, state, and national parks and forests; wildlife museums; and independent nonprofit conservation and restoration associations. Some of the many job titles a naturalist might hold are wildlife manager, fish and game warden, fish and wildlife officer, land s teward, wildlife biologist, and environmental interpreter. Natural resource managers, wildlife conservationists, and ecologists sometimes perform the work of naturalists.

HISTORY

Prior to the 17th century, there was little support for environmental preservation. Instead, wilderness was commonly seen as a vast resource to be controlled. This view began to change during the early years of the industrial revolution, when new energy resources were utilized, establishing an increasing need for petroleum, coal, natural gas, wood, and water for hydropowered energy. In England and France, for example, the rapid depletion of natural forests caused by the increased use of timber for powering the new industries led to demands for forest conservation.

The United States, especially during the 19th century, saw many of its great forests razed, huge tracts of land leveled for open-pit mining and quarrying, and increased disease with the rise of air pollution from the smokestacks of factories, home chimneys, and engine exhaust. Much of the land damage occurred at the same time as a dramatic depletion of wildlife, including elk, antelope, deer, bison, and other animals of the Great Plains. Some types of bear, cougar, and wolf became extinct, as did several kinds of birds, such as the passenger pigeon. In the latter half of the 19th century, the U.S. government set up a commission to develop scientific management of fisheries, established the first national park (Yellowstone National Park in Wyoming), and set aside the first forest reserves. The modern conservation movement grew out of these early steps.

States also established parks and forests for wilderness conservation. Parks and forests became places where people, especially urban dwellers, could acquaint themselves with the natural settings of their ancestors. Naturalists, employed by the government, institutions of higher education, and various private concerns, were involved not only in preserving and exploring the natural reserves but also in educating the public about the remaining wilderness.

Controversy over the proper role of U.S. parks and forests began soon after their creation (and continues to this day), as the value of these natural areas for logging, recreation, and other human activities conflicted with the ecological need for preservation. President Theodore Roosevelt, a strong supporter of the conservation movement, believed nevertheless in limited industrial projects, such as dams, within the wilderness areas. Despite the controversy, the system of national parks and forests expanded throughout the 20th century. Today, the Agriculture and Interior Departments, and, to a lesser extent, the Department of Defense, have conservation responsibilities for soil, forests, grasslands, water, wildlife, and federally owned land.

In the 1960s and early 1970s, the hazards posed by pollution to both humans and the environment highlighted the importance of nature preservation and public education. Federal agencies were established, such as the Environmental Protection Agency, the Council on Environmental Quality, and the National Oceanic and Atmospheric Administration. Crucial legislation was passed, including the Wilderness Act (1964) and the Endangered Species Act (1969). Naturalists have been closely involved with these conservation efforts and others, shouldering the responsibility to communicate to the public the importance of maintaining diverse ecosystems and to help restore or balance ecosystems under threat.

THE JOB

Because of the impact of human populations on the environment, virtually no area in the United States is truly wild. Land and the animal populations require human intervention to help battle against the human encroachment that is damaging or hindering wildlife. Naturalists work to help wildlife maintain or improve their hold in the world.

The work can be directly involved in maintaining individual populations of animals or plants, overseeing whole ecosystems, or promoting the work of those who are directly involved in the maintenance of the ecosystem. *Fish and wildlife officers* (or *fish and game wardens*) work to preserve and restore the animal populations, including migratory birds that may only be part of the environment temporarily. *Wildlife managers* and *range conservationists* oversee the combination of plants and animals in their territories.

Fish and wildlife officers and wardens study, assist, and help regulate the populations of fish, hunted animals, and protected animals throughout the United States. They may work directly in the parks and reserves, or they may oversee a region within a particular state, even if there are no park lands there. *Fish and game wardens* control the hunting and fishing of wild populations to make sure that the populations are not overharvested during a season. They monitor the populations of each species off season as well as make sure the species is thriving but is not overpopulating and running the risk of starvation or territory damage. Most people hear about the fish and game wardens when a population of animals has overgrown its territory and needs either to be culled (selectively hunted) or moved. Usually this occurs with the deer population, but it can also apply to predator animals such as the coyote or fox, or scavenger animals such as the raccoon. Because the practice of culling animal populations arouses controversy, the local press usually gives wide coverage to such situations.

The other common time to hear about wildlife wardens is when poaching is uncovered locally. Poaching can be hunting or fishing an animal out of season or hunting or fishing a protected animal. Although we think of poachers in the African plains hunting lions and elephants, poaching is common in the United States for animals such as mountain lions, brown bears, eagles, and wolves. Game wardens target and arrest poachers; punishment can include prison sentences and steep fines.

Wildlife managers, *range managers,* and *conservationists* work to maintain the plant and animal life in a given area. Wildlife managers can work in small local parks or enormous national parks. Range managers work on ranges that have a combination of domestic livestock and wild population. The U.S. government has leased and permitted farmers to graze and raise livestock on federally held ranges, although this program is under increasing attack by environmentalists. Range managers must ensure that both the domestic and wild populations are living side by side successfully. They make sure that the population of predatory wild animals does not increase enough to deplete the livestock and that the livestock does not overgraze the land and eliminate essential food for the wild animals. Range managers and conservationists must test soil and water for nutrients and pollution, count plant and animal populations in every season, and keep in contact with farmers using the land for reports of attacks on livestock or the presence of disease.

Wildlife managers also balance the needs of the humans using or traveling through the land they supervise and the animals that live in or travel through that same land. They keep track of the populations of animals and plants and provide food and water when it is lacking naturally. This may involve airdrops of hay and grain during winter months to deer, moose, or elk populations in remote reaches of a national forest, or digging and filling a water reservoir for animals during a drought.

Naturalists in all these positions often have administrative duties such as supervising staff members and volunteers, raising funds (particularly for independent nonprofit organizations), writing grant applications, taking and keeping records and statistics, and maintaining public relations. They may write articles for local or national publications to inform and educate the public about their location or a specific project. They may be interviewed by journalists for reports concerning their site or their work.

Nature walks are often given to groups as a way of educating people about the land and the work that goes into revitalizing and maintaining it. Tourists, schoolchildren, amateur conservationists and naturalists, social clubs, and retirees commonly attend these walks. On a nature walk, the naturalist may point out specific plants and animals, identify rocks, and discuss soil composition or the natural history of the area (including special environmental strengths and problems). The naturalist may even discuss the indigenous people of the area, especially in terms of how they adapted to the unique aspects of their particular environment. Because such a variety of topics may be brought up, the naturalist must be an environmental generalist, familiar with such subjects as biology, botany, geology, geography, meteorology, anthropology, and history.

Demonstrations, exhibits, and classes are ways that the naturalist can educate the public about the environment. For example, to help children understand oil spills, the naturalist may set up a simple demonstration showing that oil and water do not mix. Sometimes the natural setting already provides an exhibit for the naturalist. Dead fish, birds, and other animals found in a park may help demonstrate the natural life cycle and the process of decomposition. Instruction may also be given on outdoor activities, such as hiking and camping.

For some naturalists, preparing educational materials is a large part of their job. Brochures, fact sheets, pamphlets, and newsletters may be written for people visiting the park or nature center. Materials might also be sent to area residents in an effort to gain public support.

One aspect of protecting any natural area involves communicating facts and debunking myths about how to respect the area and the flora and fauna that inhabit it. Another aspect involves tending managed areas to promote a diversity of plants and animals. This may mean introducing trails and footpaths that provide easy yet noninvasive access for the public; it may mean cordoning off an area to prevent foot traffic from ruining a patch of rare moss; or it may mean instigating a letter-writing campaign to drum up support for legislation to protect a specific area, plant, or animal. It may be easy to get support for protecting the snowshoe rabbit; it is harder to make the public understand the need to preserve and maintain a batcave.

Some naturalists, such as *directors of nature centers or conservation organizations,* have massive administrative responsibilities. They might recruit volunteers and supervise staff, organize long- and short-term program goals, and handle record-keeping and the budget. To raise money, naturalists may need to speak publicly on a regular basis, write grant proposals, and organize and attend scheduled fundraising activities and community meetings. Naturalists also try to increase public awareness and support by writing press releases and organizing public workshops, conferences, seminars, meetings, and hearings. In general, naturalists must be available as resources for educating and advising the community.

REQUIREMENTS
High School
If you are interested in this field, you should take a number of basic science courses, including biology, chemistry, and Earth science. Botany courses and clubs are helpful, since they provide direct expe-

Books to Read

Baker, Nick. *The Amateur Naturalist*. Washington, D.C.: National Geographic, 2005.

Grosz, Terry. *Wildlife Wars: The Life and Times of a Fish and Game Warden*. Boulder, Colo.: Johnson Books, 1999.

National Geographic's Guide to the National Parks of the United States. 4th ed. Washington, D.C.: National Geographic, 2004.

Williams, Ernest Herbert. *The Nature Handbook: A Guide to Observing the Great Outdoors*. New York: Oxford University Press, 2005.

rience monitoring plant growth and health. Animal care experience, usually obtained through volunteer work, also is helpful. Take English courses in high school to improve your writing skills, which you will use when writing grant proposals and conducting research.

Postsecondary Training
An undergraduate degree in environmental, physical, or natural sciences is generally the minimum educational requirement for becoming a naturalist. Common college majors are biology, forestry, wildlife management, natural resource and park management, natural resources, botany, zoology, chemistry, natural history, and environmental science. Course work in economics, history, anthropology, English, international studies, and communication arts are also helpful.

Graduate education is increasingly required for employment as a naturalist, particularly for upper-level positions. A master's degree in natural science or natural resources is the minimum requirement for supervisory or administrative roles in many of the nonprofit agencies, and several positions require either a doctorate or several years of experience in the field. For positions in agencies with international sites, work abroad is necessary and can be obtained through volunteer positions such as those with the Peace Corps or in paid positions assisting in site administration and management.

Other Requirements
If you are considering a career in this field, you should like working outdoors, as most naturalists spend the majority of their time outside

in all kinds of weather. However, along with the desire to work in and with the natural world, you need to be capable of communicating with the human world as well. Excellent writing skills are helpful in preparing educational materials and grant proposals.

Seemingly unrelated skills in this field, such as engine repair and basic carpentry, can be essential to managing a post. Because of the remote locations of many of the work sites, self-sufficiency in operating and maintaining the equipment allows the staff to lose fewer days because of equipment breakdown.

EXPLORING

One of the best ways to learn about the job of a naturalist is to volunteer at one of the many national and state parks or nature centers. These institutions often recruit volunteers for outdoor work. College students, for example, are sometimes hired to work as summer or part-time nature guides. Outdoor recreation and training organizations, such as Outward Bound and the National Outdoor Leadership School, are especially good resources. Most volunteer positions, though, require a high school diploma and some college credit.

You should also consider college internship programs. In addition, conservation programs and organizations throughout the country and the world offer opportunities for volunteer work in a wide variety of areas, including working with the public, giving lectures and guided tours, and working with others to build or maintain an ecosystem. For more frequent, up-to-date information, you can read newsletters, such as *Environmental Career Opportunities* (http://ecojobs.com), that post internship and job positions. The website Environmental Career.com (http://environmental-jobs.com) also offers job listings.

EMPLOYERS

Naturalists may be employed by state agencies such as departments of wildlife, departments of fish and game, or departments of natural resources. They may work at the federal level for the U.S. Fish and Wildlife Service or the National Park Service. Naturalists may also work in the private sector for such employers as nature centers, arboretums, and botanical gardens.

STARTING OUT

If you hope to become a park employee, the usual method of entry is through part-time or seasonal employment for the first several jobs and then a full-time position. Because it is difficult to get experience before completing a college degree, and because seasonal employment is common, you should prepare to seek supplemental income for your first few years in the field.

International experience is helpful with agencies that work beyond the U.S. borders. This can be through the Peace Corps or other volunteer organizations that work with local populations on land and habitat management or restoration. Other volunteer experience is available through local restoration programs on sites in your area. Organizations such as the Nature Conservancy (http://nature.org), The Trust for Public Land (http://www.tpl.org), and many others buy land to restore, and these organizations rely extensively on volunteer labor for stewarding and working the land. Rescue and release centers work with injured and abandoned wildlife to rehabilitate them. Opportunities at these centers can include banding wild animals for tracking, working with injured or adolescent animals for release training, and adapting unreleasable animals to educational programs and presentations.

ADVANCEMENT

In some settings, such as small nature centers, there may be little room for advancement. In larger organizations, experience and additional education can lead to increased responsibility and pay. Among the higher-level positions is that of director, handling supervisory, administrative, and public relations tasks.

Advancement into upper-level management and supervisory positions usually requires a graduate degree, although people with a graduate degree and no work experience will still have to start in nearly entry-level positions. So you can either work a few years and then return to school to get an advanced degree or complete your education and start in the same position as you would have without the degree. The advanced degree will allow you eventually to move further up in the organizational structure.

EARNINGS

Earnings for naturalists are influenced by several factors, including the naturalist's specific job (for example, a wildlife biologist, a water and soil conservationist, or a game manager), the employer (for example, a state or federal agency), and the naturalist's experience and education. The U.S. Fish and Wildlife Service reports that biologists working for this department have starting salaries at the

GS-5 to GS-7 levels. In 2005, biologists at the GS-5 pay level earned annual salaries that ranged from $24,677 to $32,084, and those at the GS-7 level earned annual salaries that ranged from $30,567 to $39,738. The U.S. Fish and Wildlife Service further reports that biologists can expect to advance to GS-11 or GS-12 levels. In 2005, basic yearly pay at these levels was $45,239 and $54,221, respectively. In general, those working for state agencies have somewhat lower earnings, particularly at the entry level. And, again, the specific job a naturalist performs affects earnings. For example, the U.S. Department of Labor reports that conservation scientists had a median annual salary of $50,340 in 2002. However, some conservation workers put in 40-hour weeks and make less than $20,000 annually. As with other fields, management positions are among the highest paying. For example, in 2002, the Idaho Department of Fish and Game advertised an opening for a wildlife game manager, offering a pay range of $22.78 to $35.59 per hour. These hourly wages translate into approximately $47,380 to $74,025 per year for full-time work. Keep in mind, though, that this position and these earnings are at the top of the field. The candidate who meets the qualifications for this position would have extensive experience and be responsible for, among other things, managing research programs statewide, hiring lower-level managers, prioritizing and directing research, and acting as the department representative to other government agencies and public groups.

For some positions, housing and vehicles may be provided. Other benefits, depending on employer, may include health insurance, vacation time, and retirement plans.

WORK ENVIRONMENT

Field naturalists spend a majority of their working hours outdoors. Depending on the location, the naturalist must work in a wide variety of weather conditions: from frigid cold to sweltering heat to torrential rain. Remote sites are common, and long periods of working either in isolation or in small teams is not uncommon for field research and management. Heavy lifting, hauling, working with machinery and hand tools, digging, planting, harvesting, and tracking may fall to the naturalist working in the field. One wildlife manager in Montana spent every daylight hour for several days in a row literally running up and down snow-covered mountains, attempting to tranquilize and collar a mountain lion. Clearly, this can be a physically demanding job.

Indoor work includes scheduling, planning, and classroom teaching. Data gathering and maintaining logs and records are required for many jobs. Naturalists may need to attend and speak at local community meetings. They may have to read detailed legislative bills to analyze the impact of legislation before it becomes law.

Those in supervisory positions, such as directors, are often so busy with administrative and organizational tasks that they may spend little of their workday outdoors. Work that includes guided tours and walks through nature areas is frequently seasonal and usually dependent on daily visitors.

Full-time naturalists usually work about 35 to 40 hours per week. Overtime is often required, and for those naturalists working in areas visited by campers, camping season is extremely busy and can require much overtime. Wildlife and range managers may be on call during storms and severe weather. Seasonal work, such as burn season for land managers and stewards, may require overtime and frequent weekend work.

Naturalists have special occupational hazards, such as working with helicopters, small airplanes, all-terrain vehicles, and other modes of transport through rugged landscapes and into remote regions. Adverse weather conditions and working in rough terrain make illness and injury more likely. Naturalists must be able to get along with the variety of people using the area and may encounter armed individuals who are poaching or otherwise violating the law.

Naturalists also have a number of unique benefits. Most prominent is the chance to live and work in some of the most beautiful places in the world. For many individuals, the lower salaries are offset by the recreational and lifestyle opportunities afforded by living and working in such scenic areas. In general, occupational stress is low, and most naturalists appreciate the opportunity to continually learn about and work to improve the environment.

OUTLOOK

The outlook for naturalists is expected to be fair in the first decade of the 21st century. While a growing public concern about environmental issues may cause an increased demand for naturalists, this trend could be offset by government cutbacks in funding for nature programs. Reduced government spending on education may indirectly affect the demand for naturalists, as school districts would have less money to spend on outdoor education and recreation. Despite the limited number of available positions, the number of well-qualified applicants is expected to remain high.

FOR MORE INFORMATION

For information on environmental expeditions, contact
Earthwatch Institute
3 Clock Tower Place, Suite 100
PO Box 75
Maynard, MA 01754
Tel: 800-776-0188
Email: info@earthwatch.org
http://www.earthwatch.org

For information about internships, career conferences, and publications, contact
Environmental Careers Organization
30 Winter Street
Boston, MA 02108
Tel: 617-426-4375
http://www.eco.org

This group offers internships and fellowships for college and graduate students with an interest in environmental issues. For information, contact
Friends of the Earth
1717 Massachusetts Avenue, NW, 600
Washington, DC 20036-2002
Tel: 877-843-8687
Email: foe@foe.org
http://www.foe.org

For information on a variety of conservation programs, contact
National Wildlife Federation
11100 Wildlife Center Drive
Reston, VA 20190-5362
Tel: 800-822-9919
http://www.nwf.org

For information on volunteer opportunities, contact
Student Conservation Association
689 River Road
PO Box 550
Charlestown, NC 03603-0550
Tel: 603-543-1700
http://www.sca-inc.org

For information on careers, contact
U.S. Fish and Wildlife Service
U.S. Department of the Interior
Division of Human Resources
4401 North Fairfax Drive, Mailstop: 2000
Arlington, VA 22203
http://hr.fws.gov/HR/Careers_FWS.htm

For information on federal employment, contact
USAJOBS
Office of Personnel Management
http://www.usajobs.opm.gov

Oceanographers

OVERVIEW

Oceanographers obtain information about the ocean through observations, surveys, and experiments. They study the biological, physical, and chemical composition of the ocean and the geological structure of the seabed. They also analyze phenomena involving the water itself, the atmosphere above it, the land beneath it, and the coastal borders. They study acoustical properties of water so that a comprehensive and unified picture of the ocean's behavior may be developed. A *limnologist* is a specialist who studies freshwater life.

HISTORY

The oceans hold approximately 97 percent of the water on Earth and cover more than two-thirds of its surface. Oceans hold food, chemicals, and minerals, yet oceanography is a fairly new science. In fact, according to the Oceanography Society, it was only during the 20th century that we got the first global glimpse of how the oceans work. With such inventions as deep-sea diving gear, scuba, and the bathysphere (a steel diving sphere for deep-sea observation), scientists are undertaking more detailed studies of underwater life. Oceanography includes studying air and sea interaction in weather forecasting, solving sea mining problems, predicting and preventing pollution, studying sea life, and improving methods of deriving foods from the ocean.

It is difficult to project what oceanographers of the future may be doing. They may be living and working on the ocean floor. The U.S. Navy Medical Research Laboratory has conducted experiments with people living under 200 feet of water.

THE JOB

Oceanographers collect and study data about the motions of ocean water (waves, currents, and tides), marine life (sea plants and animals), ore and petroleum deposits (minerals and oils contained in the nodules and oozes of the ocean floor), and the contour of the ocean floor (ocean mountains, valleys, and depths). Many of their findings are compiled for maps, charts, graphs, and special reports and manuals.

Oceanographers may spend some of their time on the water each year gathering data and making observations. Additional oceanographic work is done on dry land by people who infrequently go to sea. Experiments using models or captive organisms may be conducted in the seaside laboratory.

Oceanographers use equipment designed and manufactured in special shops. This equipment includes devices to measure depths by sound impulses, special thermometers to measure water temperatures, special cameras for underwater photography, and diving gear and machines like the bathyscaphe (a submersible ship for deep-sea exploration). In addition to such commonly used equipment, many new devices have been developed for specific types of underwater work. The oceanographer of the future may be using such tools as a hydraulic miner (a dredge to extract nodules from the ocean floor), an electronic beater (a machine used to drive fish), dye curtains, fish pumps, and instrument buoys. New technologies being developed today include satellite sensors and acoustic current-measuring devices.

The oceanographer is usually part of a highly skilled team, with each member specializing in one of the four main branches of the profession. In actual work, however, there is a tremendous amount of overlap between the four branches. *Biological oceanographers* or *marine biologists* study all aspects of the ocean's plant and animal life. They are interested in how the life develops, interacts, and adapts to its environment. *Physical oceanographers* study such physical aspects of the ocean as temperature and density, waves and currents, and the relationship between the ocean and the atmosphere. *Chemical oceanographers* and *marine geochemists* investigate the chemical composition of the water and ocean floor. They may study seawater components, pollutants, and trace chemicals, which are small amounts of dissolved substances that give an area of water a specific quality. *Geological oceanographers* study the topographic features and physical composition of the ocean bottom. Their work greatly contributes to our knowledge and understanding of Earth's history.

Oceanography jobs can be found all over the United States, and not just where the water meets the shore. Although the majority of jobs are on the Pacific, Atlantic, and Gulf coasts, many other jobs are

Did You Know?

- Oceans cover nearly three-quarters of the planet's surface—336 million cubic miles.
- Ocean depth averages 2.3 miles. The greatest known depth of any ocean is in the Challenger Deep of the Mariana Trench in the Pacific Ocean, about 250 miles southwest of Guam. Recorded echo soundings indicate a maximum depth of about 36,000 feet.
- The ocean's intricate food webs support more life by weight and a greater diversity of animals than any other ecosystem.
- The oceans have vast reserves of commercially valuable minerals, including nickel, iron, manganese, copper, and cobalt.
- The surface temperature of oceans ranges from about 86°F at the equator to about 29°F near the poles. The world's warmest water is in the Persian Gulf, where surface temperatures of 96°F have been recorded.

available to the marine scientist. Universities, colleges, and federal and state agencies are the largest employers of oceanographers. Mary Batteen is the chairperson of the oceanography department at the Naval Postgraduate School in Monterey, California, a professor in the department, and a working oceanographer. She has many job responsibilities. "As the chairperson," she says, " I interact regularly with a variety of people: my office staff, faculty, technical staff (usually oceanographers with M.S. degrees), other chairs, the dean, the provost, and many students. I am responsible for making sure that the oceanography department runs smoothly. As a faculty member, I regularly interact with students when I teach, advise theses, or carry out joint research with them. My major research interest is understanding the coastal circulation off west coasts like California, Portugal, Morocco, Chile, and Western Australia. Typical research questions I pursue are: Why, at the same latitude, is the water warm off Western Australia and cool off the other west coasts? Why do some coastal currents flow opposite to the prevailing winds? What roles do wind forcing, capes (bays), and bottom topography play in causing eddies to develop off west coasts? To address these questions, I use a combination of numerical models and available ocean observations."

Other employers of oceanographers include international organizations, private companies, consulting firms, nonprofit laboratories, and local governments. Sometimes oceanographers are self-employed as consultants with their own businesses.

REQUIREMENTS

High School

Because a college degree is required for beginning positions in oceanography, you should take four years of college preparatory courses while in high school. Science courses, including geology, biology, and chemistry, and math classes, such as algebra, trigonometry, and statistics, are especially important to take. Because your work will involve a great deal of research and documentation, take English classes to improve your research and communication skills. In addition, take computer science classes because you will be using computers throughout your professional life.

Postsecondary Training

In college, a broad program covering the basic sciences with a major in physics, chemistry, biology, or geology is desirable. In addition, you should include courses in field research or laboratory work in oceanography where available. Graduate work in oceanography is required for most positions in research and teaching. More than 100 institutions offer programs in marine studies, and more than 35 universities have graduate programs leading to a doctoral degree in oceanography.

As a college student preparing for graduate work in oceanography, you should take mathematics through differential and integral calculus and at least one year each of chemistry and physics, biology or geology, and a modern foreign language.

Many oceanography students participate in internships or work as teaching assistants while in college to gain hands on experience in the field. Mary Batteen was a graduate teaching assistant while pursuing her M.S. degree in oceanography. "Besides learning to teach," she says, "I learned on-the-job skills while out on oceanography cruises. While pursuing my Ph.D. I was a graduate research assistant. I learned many computer skills while analyzing oceanographic data and running numerical models."

Other Requirements

Personal traits helpful to a career in oceanography are a strong interest in science, particularly the physical and earth sciences; an interest in situations involving activities of an abstract and creative nature (observing nature, performing experiments, creating objects); an interest in outdoor activities such as hunting, fishing, swimming, boating, or animal care; an interest in scholarly activities (reading, researching, writing); and other interests that cut across the traditional academic boundaries of biology, chemistry, and physics.

You should have above-average aptitudes in verbal, numerical, and spatial abilities. Prospective oceanographers should also be able to discriminate detail among objects in terms of their shape, size, color, or markings.

EXPLORING

Obviously, if you live near coastal regions, you will have an easier time becoming familiar with oceans and ocean life than if you are land-bound. However, some institutions offer work or leisure-time experiences that provide participants with opportunities to explore particular aspects of oceanography. Possible opportunities include work in marine or conservation fisheries or on board seagoing vessels or field experiences in studying rocks, minerals, or aquatic life. If you live or travel near one of the oceanography research centers, such as Woods Hole Oceanographic Institution on Cape Cod, the University of Miami's Rosenstiel School of Marine and Atmospheric Science, or the Scripps Institution of Oceanography in California, you should plan to spend some time learning about their activities and studying their exhibits.

Volunteer work for students is often available with research teams, nonprofit organizations, and public centers such as aquariums. If you do not live near water, try to find summer internships, camps, or programs that involve travel to a coastal area. You can help pave your way into the field by learning all you can about the geology, atmosphere, and plant and animal life of the area where you live, regardless of whether water is present.

EMPLOYERS

Nearly 50 percent of those working in oceanography and marine-related fields work for federal or state governments. Federal employers of oceanographers, ocean engineers, marine technicians, and those interested in marine policy include the Department of Defense, the Environmental Protection Agency, the U.S. Geological Survey, and the National Biological Survey, among others. State governments often employ oceanographers in environmental agencies or state-funded research projects.

Forty percent of oceanographers are employed by colleges or universities, where they teach, conduct research, write, and consult. The remaining 10 percent of oceanographers work for private industries such as oil companies and nonprofit organizations, including environmental societies. An increasing number of oceanographers are being employed each year by industrial firms, particularly those involved in oceanographic instrument and equipment manufacturing, shipbuilding, and chemistry.

STARTING OUT

Most college placement offices are staffed to help you find positions in business and industry after you graduate. Often positions can be found through friends, relatives, or college professors or through the college's career service's office by application and interview. College and university assistantships, instructorships, and professorships are usually obtained by recommendation of your major professor or department chairperson. In addition, internships with the government or private industry during college can often lead to permanent employment after graduation. The American Institute of Biological Sciences maintains an employment service and lists both employers and job seekers.

ADVANCEMENT

Starting oceanography positions usually involve working as a laboratory or research assistant, with on-the-job training in applying oceanographic principles to the problems at hand. Some beginning oceanographers with Ph.D.'s may qualify for college teaching or research positions. Experienced personnel, particularly those with advanced graduate work or doctorates, can become supervisors or administrators. Such positions involve considerable responsibility in planning and policymaking or policy interpretation. Those who achieve top-level oceanographer positions may plan and supervise research projects involving a number of workers, or they may be in charge of an oceanographic laboratory or aquarium.

EARNINGS

While marine scientists are richly rewarded in nonmaterial ways for their diverse and exciting work with the sea, they almost never become wealthy by American standards. Salaries depend on education, experience, and chosen discipline. Supply and demand issues along with where you work also come into play. Some examples of jobs in the marine sciences that presently pay more than the average include physical oceanography, marine technology and engineering, and computer modeling.

According to a 2003 report by the National Association of Colleges and Employers, students graduating with a bachelor's degree in geology and geological sciences were offered an average starting salary of $32,828. Graduates with a master's degree started at an average of $47,981; with a doctoral degree, $61,050.

According to the *Occupational Outlook Handbook,* in 2003, salaries for geoscientists (which includes geologists, geophysicists, and oceanographers) ranged from less than $37,690 to more than $131,510, with a median of $68,570. The average salary for experienced oceanographers working for the federal government was $79,023 in 2003.

In addition to their regular salaries, oceanographers may supplement their incomes with fees earned from consulting, lecturing, and publishing their findings. As highly trained scientists, oceanographers usually enjoy good benefits, such as health insurance and retirement plans offered by their employers.

WORK ENVIRONMENT

Oceanographers in shore stations, laboratories, and research centers work five-day, 40-hour weeks. Occasionally, they serve a longer shift, particularly when a research experiment demands around-the-clock surveillance. Such assignments may also involve unusual working hours, depending on the nature of the research or the purpose of the trip. Trips at sea mean time away from home for periods extending from a few days to several months. Sea expeditions may be physically demanding and present an entirely different way of life: living on board a ship. Weather conditions may impose some hazards during these assignments. Choosing to engage in underwater research may mean a more adventuresome and hazardous way of life than in other occupations. It is wise to discover early whether or not life at sea appeals to you so that you may pursue appropriate jobs within the oceanography field.

Many jobs in oceanography, however, exist in laboratories, offices, and aquariums, with little time spent underwater or at sea. Many oceanographers are needed to analyze samples brought to land from sea; to plan, develop, and organize seafaring trips from land; and to teach. Oceanographers who work in colleges or universities get the added benefit of the academic calendar, which provides time off for travel or research.

OUTLOOK

The U.S. Department of Labor expects employment for oceanographers to grow about as fast as the average through 2012.

Although the field of marine science is growing, researchers specializing in the popular field of biological oceanography, or marine biology, will face competition for available positions and research funding over the next few years. However, funding for graduate students and professional positions is expected to increase during the coming decade in the areas of global climate change, environmental research and management, fisheries science, and marine biomedical and pharmaceutical research programs. Although job availability is difficult to predict for several years out, anyone doing good, strong academic work with a well-known professor in the field has good employment chances.

In the late 1990s, the largest demand in oceanography and marine-related fields was for physical and chemical oceanographers and ocean engineers, according to The Oceanographic Society. Demand and supply, however, are difficult to predict and can change according to the world market situation; for example, the state of the offshore oil market can affect demand for geological and geophysical oceanographers.

The growth of technology will continue to create and expand job opportunities for those interested in the marine sciences. As ways of collecting and analyzing data become more advanced, many more research positions are opening up for microbiologists, geneticists, and biochemists, fields that were limited by the capabilities of past technology but are now rapidly expanding. All these fields can have ties to the marine biological sciences. In general, oceanographers who also have training in other sciences or in engineering will probably have better opportunities for employment than those with training limited to oceanography.

The Oceanography Society says the growing interest in understanding and protecting the environment will also create new jobs. Careers related to fisheries resources, including basic research in biology and chemistry, as well as mariculture and sea ranching, will also increase. Because the oceans hold vast resources of commercially valuable minerals, employment opportunities will come from pharmaceutical and biotechnology companies and others interested in mining these substances for potential "miracle drugs" and other commercial uses. Continued deep-sea exploration made possible by underwater robotics and autonomous seacraft may also create more market opportunities for underwater research, with perhaps more international than U.S.-based employment potential.

FOR MORE INFORMATION

For education and career information, contact the following organizations:

Acoustical Society of America
2 Huntington Quadrangle, Suite 1NO1
Melville, NY 11747-4502
Tel: 516-576-2360
Email: asa@aip.org
http://asa.aip.org

American Geophysical Union
2000 Florida Avenue, NW
Washington, DC 20009-1277
Tel: 800-966-2481
Email: service@agu.org
http://www.agu.org

The education and outreach section of the AIBS website has information on a number of careers in biology.

American Institute of Biological Sciences (AIBS)
1444 I Street, NW, Suite 200
Washington, DC 20005
Tel: 202-628-1500
Email: admin@aibs.org
http://www.aibs.org

Visit the ASLO's website for information on careers and education. For information on membership and publications, contact

American Society of Limnology and Oceanography (ASLO)
5400 Bosque Boulevard, Suite 680
Waco, TX 76710-4446
Tel: 800-929-2756
Email: business@aslo.org
http://www.aslo.org

For information about ocean careers and education, contact

Department of Oceanography
Texas A&M University
3146 TAMU
College Station, TX 77843-3146
Tel: 979-845-7211
http://www-ocean.tamu.edu

To purchase the booklet Education and Training Programs in Oceanography and Related Fields, *contact*
Marine Technology Society (MTS)
5565 Sterrett Place, Suite 108
Columbia, MD 21044
Tel: 410-884-5330
http://www.mtsociety.org

Contact this society for ocean news and information on membership.
The Oceanography Society
PO Box 1931
Rockville, MD 20849-1931
Tel: 301-251-7708
Email: info@tos.org
http://www.tos.org

For information on undergraduate and graduate programs available at Scripps Institution of Oceanography, contact
Scripps Institution of Oceanography
University of California, San Diego
9500 Gilman Drive, 0233
La Jolla, CA 92093-0233
Tel: 858-534-3624
Email: scrippsnews@ucsd.edu
http://www-sio.ucsd.edu

The IEEE Oceanic Engineering Society is a technical society of the Institute of Electrical and Electronics Engineering. The OES Newsletter, with information on the field, can be read online at the website.
IEEE Oceanic Engineering Society
http://www.oceanicengineering.org

The Scripps Institution of Oceanography Library provides numerous links to career information at this website.
Careers in Oceanography, Marine Science, and Marine Biology
http://scilib.ucsd.edu/sio/guide/career.html

Pharmacologists

QUICK FACTS

School Subjects
Biology
Chemistry
Mathematics

Personal Skills
Communication/ideas
Technical/scientific

Work Environment
Primarily indoors
Primarily one location

Minimum Education Level
Doctorate degree

Salary Range
$55,000 to $97,600 to
$120,500+

Certification or Licensing
Voluntary

Outlook
Faster than the average

DOT
041

GOE
02.03.01

NOC
2121

O*NET-SOC
19-1042.00

OVERVIEW

Pharmacologists play an important role in medicine and in science by studying the effects of drugs, chemicals, and other substances on humans, animals, and plants. These highly educated scientists conduct research on living tissues and organs to determine how drugs and other chemicals act at the cellular level. Their results help to discover how drugs and other chemicals should be most effectively used. The study of pharmacology is necessary to standardize drug dosages; analyze chemicals, food additives, poisons, insecticides, and other substances; and identify dangerous substances and harmful levels of controlled chemicals.

HISTORY

Pharmacology is not the same as pharmacy. Pharmacology is the science concerned with the interactions between chemicals and biological systems. Pharmacy is the practice of preparation and dispensing of drugs to patients.

Past civilizations, especially the cultures of ancient Greece and China, compiled the earliest written pharmacological knowledge, identifying certain diseases and the recommended "prescriptions" for these ailments. It was not until thousands of years later that organized experiments in pharmacology began. Many credit Francois Magendie, an early 19th-century French physiologist, with the birth of experimental pharmacology. The research of Magendie and his student, Claude Bernard, on poisons such as strychnine and carbon monoxide, and on the use of curare as a muscle relaxant, helped to establish many of the principles of modern pharmacology. In 1847, a German, Rudolf Bucheim, started the first institute of pharmacology at the University of Dorpat, establishing the study of pharmacology as a singular discipline. A student of Bucheim, Oswald Schmiedeberg, became a professor of pharmacology and further passed on his knowledge to students from all over the world. One of these students, John Jacob Abel, is credited with bringing experimental pharmacology to the United States.

The medical achievements and discoveries of pharmacologists are numerous. Their work has helped in the development of antibiotics, anesthetics, vaccines, tranquilizers, vitamins, and many other substances in wide medical use today. Pharmacologists have been instrumental, for example, in the use of ether and other anesthetics that have modernized surgical procedures. Their research was used in the development of lifesaving drugs such as penicillin, tetanus and polio vaccines, antimalaria drugs, and countless other compounds. In addition, pharmacologists have helped to develop drugs to treat heart disease, cancer, and psychiatric illnesses.

With the scientific advances of the early 20th century, especially the introduction of antibacterial drugs into medicine, pharmacology gained recognition as a distinct discipline. Spurred by pharmacological research, the Food, Drug, and Cosmetic Act of 1938 was introduced, requiring rigorous studies of drugs before they could be marketed. Regulations continue today through the Food and Drug Administration.

Unlike early pharmacologists who were strictly devoted to developing new drugs, modern pharmacologists perform a much broader range of activities. They test pesticides for harmful reactions, identify poisons and their effects, analyze industrial pollutants, study food preservatives and colorings, and check other substances for their effects on the environment as well as on humans. Their research includes all aspects of modern molecular and cellular biology as well as effects of drugs in animals and humans.

THE JOB

Pharmacologists are highly trained scientists who study the effects drugs and other chemical agents have on humans, animals, and plants. They may create new drugs, test old drugs for new uses, or study the interaction between drugs or other chemical agents on an organism to find out how a disease progresses. Pharmacologists perform research in laboratories using cultured cells, laboratory animals, plants, human tissues, precision electronic instruments, and computers. They try to answer such questions as: What is a drug's effect on the cellular system of the tissue or other subject being studied?

How is the drug absorbed, distributed, and released from the cells or organism? Are the cells or organism developing sensitivity to the drug and how is that happening? Pharmacology also involves studying therapeutics and toxicology as they relate to drugs and other chemical agents. *Therapeutics* refers to the drugs or other agents' action or influence on diseases as well as the diseases' influence on the properties of drugs and other agents. Pharmacologists specializing in drug research, for example, may study the therapeutic effects of medical compounds on specific organs or bodily systems. They identify potentially beneficial and potentially harmful side effects and are then able to predict the drug's usefulness against specific diseases. They also use this information to recommend proper dosages and describe circumstances in which a drug should be administered. *Toxicology* refers to the toxic effects of drugs used to treat diseases as well as the toxic effects of chemical agents in the environment, agriculture, and industry. Pharmacologists trying to identify if there is a hazardous substance in an environment that is making people ill, for example, are involved in toxicology. They may analyze chemicals to determine if dangerous amounts of lead, mercury, or ammonia are in workplaces, pesticides, food preservatives, or even common household items such as paints, aerosol sprays, and cleaning fluids.

The complex field of pharmacology is divided into several areas in which pharmacologists may choose to specialize. *Neuropharmacologists* focus on drugs relating to the nervous system, including the brain, spinal cord, and nerves. *Cardiovascular pharmacologists* specialize in the effects of drugs relating to the cardiovascular and circulatory systems. *Endocrine pharmacologists* study drug effects on the hormonal balance of the body. *Molecular pharmacologists* study the biochemical and biophysical interactions between drug molecules and cells. *Biochemical pharmacologists* use biochemistry, cell biology, and physiology to determine how drugs interact and influence the chemical makeup of an organism. *Veterinary pharmacologists* are experts on the use and study of drugs with animals. *Behavioral pharmacologists,* sometimes known as *psychopharmacologists,* specialize in studying drugs that affect such things as behavior patterns, learning processes, and mental illnesses. *Chemotherapy pharmacologists* focus their work on creating drugs that will stop the growth of or kill infectious agents or cancer cells without harming healthy cells. *Clinical pharmacologists* specialize in studying how various drugs and chemical compounds work only in human subjects.

Because this work is so complex, requiring knowledge of many aspects of different sciences, mathematics, and even technology, it is not uncommon for teams of pharmacologists to work together, especially in the development of more complex drugs and compounds capable of treating numerous diseases. Pharmacologists may work for laboratories of pharmaceutical companies or universities. A number also teach at universities or medical schools. Research projects take considerable time to complete. In general, it takes 10 years for pharmacologists to develop, test, and refine a new drug product before the Food and Drug Administration will approve its use for the public. Throughout this entire process, pharmacologists must pay strict attention to detail and keep accurate documentation.

Dr. Dennis Mungall is the director of clinical pharmacology and anticoagulation services at a family practice residency. His clinical research involves cardiovascular medicine and coagulation disorders. He also works as a teacher, helping physicians-in-training, pharmacy students, and general health care providers understand drug therapies and side effects. "I teach how to streamline care," he says, "so that it's cost-effective and easy for the patients. I teach them how to pick the best therapy that fits the patient's pathology. Drug-drug interactions can cause adverse effects; I teach how to understand these and how to avoid them." Mungall says this work is a science of tailoring drug therapy to the individual patient.

REQUIREMENTS
High School
It takes many years of education to become a pharmacologist, but you can begin to prepare yourself for this work by taking college prep classes while in high school. Naturally, you should take science courses, including biology, chemistry, and physics. If your school offers more advanced science courses, such as molecular biology and organic chemistry, take these as well. You will also need a strong math background, so take four years of mathematics, including algebra, geometry, statistics, trigonometry, pre-calculus, and calculus, if your school offers this. Keep your computer skills up to date by taking computer science classes. Because you will need strong researching, writing, and speaking skills, you should also take four years of English classes.

Postsecondary Training
Your next step after high school is to earn an undergraduate degree. A few universities offer an undergraduate degree in pharmacology. Because of the limited number of schools offering this degree, however, many students choose to get bachelor's degrees in chemistry or a biological science, which are also appropriate. No matter what

your major is, your college studies should again focus on sciences (biologies, physics, organic and inorganic chemistry) and mathematics (such as differential calculus and integral calculus). Other courses to take include English, computer science, and a foreign language.

After college, you need to complete graduate-level work. To conduct research, teach at a medical school or school of pharmacy, or advance to high level administrative positions, the minimum education you need is a doctorate degree in pharmacology. Many pharmacologists, however, have more than one advanced degree. Some, for example, have a doctorate in another science, such as biochemistry, and a doctorate in pharmacology. Others have medical degrees (M.D.'s) and pharmacology doctorates. Some pharmacologists who specialize in animal pharmacology are also doctors of veterinary medicine (D.V.M.'s). Many courses in pharmacology closely resemble medical school courses, and Ph.D.'s in pharmacology are offered at medical schools, schools of pharmacy, and research universities. Certain veterinary schools offer degrees in veterinary pharmacology as well.

The American Society for Pharmacology and Experimental Therapeutics, a professional organization of pharmacologists, provides a list of accredited pharmacology graduate programs as well as other relevant information. (Visit the Training Programs section on its website, http://www.aspet.org.) Once you've been accepted to such an institution, the Ph.D. program generally takes between four to six years to complete. Studies involve intensive courses in cellular and molecular biology, physiology, neuroscience, basic and molecular pharmacology, chemotherapy, toxicology, statistics, and research. The major portion of the Ph.D. program requires students to undertake independent and supervised research and successfully complete an original laboratory project. Graduate students must also write a doctoral thesis on their research project.

After receiving their Ph.D., many pharmacologists go on to complete two to four additional years of postdoctoral research training in which they assist a scientist on a second project in order to gain further research skills, experience, and maturity.

Certification or Licensing

Pharmacologists may choose to become certified within a special area of study. The Board of Clinical Pharmacology, for example, offers certification in clinical and applied pharmacology. Applicants are judged based on training and experience. They must first receive their doctoral degree and complete at least five years of postdoctoral work in clinical pharmacology, among other requirements, before being eligible for the exam.

Other Requirements

"Communication is the most important part of the job," says Dr. Dennis Mungall. "You'll be organizing patients, administrators, people in business, and others—bringing people together for projects." Mungall also emphasizes creativity. "Being creative," he says, "adds to your ability to be a good researcher, to be a good thinker."

Pharmacologists must be creative, curious, and flexible in order to entertain new ideas or investigative strategies. They need to be patient and willing to work long hours in order to master research that does not provide quick or easy answers. They must also be able to work alone or with similarly dedicated and driven colleagues to the conclusion of a project.

EXPLORING

The best way to learn about pharmacology is to interview professionals in the career. Your high school counselor or science teacher may be able to arrange an interview with a qualified pharmacologist or even help plan a tour of a pharmacological facility.

Contact professional organizations for information about this career. The American Society for Pharmacology and Experimental Therapeutics provides information on the field of pharmacology, including educational programs and academic institutions, the various subspecialties of pharmacology, and laboratories, drug companies, and other branches of the profession that employ pharmacologists.

Medical and other laboratories frequently employ part-time personnel to assist with various tasks. Information regarding summer or part-time opportunities can be obtained by contacting work-study or student research programs and student placement services. But you need to keep in mind that these positions can be hard to come by because you may be competing with pharmacological graduate students for jobs. If you are unable to get one of these positions, consider getting any type of work or experience that will give you the opportunity to be in a laboratory or medical setting. For example, you may be able to volunteer at a local hospital's pharmacy or find part-time work at a doctor's office. While you may be filing papers and updating computer records, you will also be learning about various drugs and what they do.

Books to Read

Edmunds, Marilyn W. *Introduction to Clinical Pharmacology.* 4th ed. St. Louis: Mosby, 2002.

Mycek, Mary Julia, Richard A. Harvey, and Pamela C. Champe, eds. *Lippincott's Illustrated Reviews: Pharmacology: Special Millennium Update.* 2d ed. Philadelphia: Lippincott Williams & Wilkins, 2000.

Springhouse Staff. *Clinical Pharmacology Made Incredibly Easy.* Philadelphia: Lippincott Williams & Wilkins, 2000.

Stringer, Janet L. *Basic Concepts in Pharmacology: A Student's Survival Guide.* 2d ed. New York: Appleton & Lange, 2000.

Woodrow, Ruth. *Essentials of Pharmacology in Health Occupations.* 4th ed. Clifton Park, N.Y.: Delmar Thomson Learning, 2001.

EMPLOYERS

Pharmacologists are employed as faculty in medical, dental, veterinary, or pharmacy schools, and as researchers in large hospitals, medical centers, or research institutes. They also work for government agencies involved in research such as the National Institutes of Health, the Environmental Protection Agency, and the Food and Drug Administration.

STARTING OUT

Drug companies, research organizations, medical, dental, and pharmacy schools and universities, and federal and state governments often recruit pharmacologists while they are in the process of earning their doctorates. By the second year of their doctoral program, most pharmacologists have chosen a subspecialty and seek out employers representing their chosen area.

If you have not taken a job with an organization recruiting on your campus, you should be able to consult your school's placement office for job leads. If there are research institutes or pharmaceutical and chemical companies of interest to you, you can send resumes directly to them. Additionally, pharmacological journals often list job openings, and professional organizations usually provide employment services or news.

ADVANCEMENT

Most beginning pharmacologists start out in academics at the assistant professor level or work in laboratories, assisting advanced pharmacologists in research. Beginning pharmacologists work to improve their laboratory procedures, learn how to work with the Food and Drug Administration and various other government agencies, and gain experience testing drugs and other substances on both animal and human subjects. In research institutes, private industry, and academic laboratories, advancement in the field of pharmacology usually means moving into a supervising position, overseeing other scientists in a laboratory setting and heading up major research projects. Pharmacologists who work as teachers advance by serving as department heads, supervising research laboratories at universities, presenting public papers, and speaking at major conferences.

Pharmacologists often view their advancements in terms of successful research projects. Dr. Dennis Mungall is looking forward to branching out into other areas to combine his interests in pharmacology, writing, and the Internet. "I have a grant from the American Heart Association to do just that," he says, "using the Internet to improve health care communication with patients."

EARNINGS

A 2001 survey (the most recent information available) by the American Association of Pharmaceutical Scientists places average base salaries (excluding bonuses) for pharmacologists at $97,600 a year for those working in industry, $95,100 for those in academia, and $81,400 for those in government. The survey also compared salaries by education level and work experience. Pharmacologists with a master's degree and 0 to 5 years of experience earned annual mean salaries of $55,000; with 10 to 20 years, $76,000; and 30 or more years, $106,000. Pharmacologists with a Ph.D. and 0 to 5 years of experience earned annual mean salaries of $72,000; with 10 to 20 years, $108,000; and 30 or more years, $120,500. Bonuses, especially for those in industry, can increase yearly earnings considerably.

Benefits generally include health and dental insurance and paid vacation and sick days.

WORK ENVIRONMENT

Pharmacologists work in academic settings or laboratories and generally work 40 hours a week, though they may sometimes be required to work extra hours to monitor experiments that need special attention. Most laboratories associated with academic or major research institutions are clean, well-lit, pleasant workplaces equipped with the sophisticated instruments necessary for modern research. Because pharmacologists perform such a vital role with respect to drug and chemical research, their laboratories tend to be fairly up-to-date.

Pharmacologists often work on projects that require years of effort and may for months show seemingly little progress. Pharmacologists must be able to deal with other professionals during what can be frustrating times as research and experiments do not go as planned. They must also be able to deal with the potential stresses associated with working in close quarters with others, sharing laboratory space or other resources.

In some cases, pharmacologists are called upon to work with forensic biologists, coroners, or others involved in determining causes of death under specific circumstances. They may also be asked to travel to other research institutions to share their findings.

OUTLOOK

Although the U.S. Department of Labor does not provide information on pharmacologists, it does recognize the related position of medical scientist (scientists involved with researching the causes of diseases and finding treatments for these diseases). The department predicts the employment outlook for medical scientists to be faster than the average through 2012, although competition for jobs will be extremely keen. This is because research work is dependent on funding, typically from government sources. In recent years government cutbacks have limited the amount of funding available and, thus, limited research and work opportunities. Pharmacologists, who are also dependent on funding for research projects, are likely to face this same stiff competition for money and jobs. So while the employment outlook overall is good, only those with the most advanced and updated education will have the best prospects in future expanding and specialized job markets.

Areas in which growth is expected include health care, education, and research. Expanding health care needs and services should result in employment opportunities for pharmacologists in drug companies, hospitals, and medical and pharmacy schools. Pharmacological research done by government agencies will also continue.

Teaching opportunities should be plentiful as schools, universities, and medical centers will need qualified pharmacologists to train future students.

The growing elderly population will require pharmacologists to conduct more drug research and development. Pharmacology is also crucial in the development of drugs to battle existing diseases and medical conditions such as AIDS, muscular dystrophy, and cancer, and to facilitate the success of organ transplants.

Further study into drug addiction, gene therapy, and the effect of chemical substances on the environment, including their relationship to cancer and birth defects, will also provide research opportunities for qualified pharmacologists. The increasing interest in more non-traditional medical treatments will also open doors to pharmacologists in such subspecialties as herbal pharmacology, which focuses on the medicinal values of plants.

FOR MORE INFORMATION

To learn more about pharmacology and read news of interest to those in the field, visit the AAPS website.
 American Association of Pharmaceutical Scientists (AAPS)
 2107 Wilson Boulevard, Suite 700
 Arlington, VA 22201-3042
 Tel: 703-243-2800
 Email: aaps@aaps.org
 http://www.aapspharmaceutica.com

For information on certification, contact
 American Board of Clinical Pharmacology
 PO Box 40278
 San Antonio, TX 78229-1278
 Tel: 210-567-8505
 http://www.abcp.net

For information on undergraduate and graduate programs in pharmacology, the online publication Explore Pharmacology, *and a career center for students, visit the ASPET website.*
 American Society for Pharmacology and Experimental
 Therapeutics (ASPET)
 9650 Rockville Pike
 Bethesda, MD 20814-3995
 Tel: 301-530-7060
 Email: info@aspet.org
 http://www.aspet.org

Toxicologists

OVERVIEW

Toxicologists design and conduct studies to determine the potential toxicity of substances to humans, plants, and animals. They provide information on the hazards of these substances to the federal government, private businesses, and the public. Toxicologists may suggest alternatives to using products that contain dangerous amounts of toxins, often by testifying at official hearings. There are an estimated 9,000 toxicologists currently employed in the United States.

HISTORY

The study of the effects of poisons (toxins) began in the 1500s, when doctors documented changes in body tissues of people who died after a long illness. Although research was hampered by the lack of sophisticated research equipment, physicians and scientists continued to collect information on the causes and effects of various diseases over the next 300 years.

As microscopes and other forms of scientific equipment improved, scientists were able to study in greater detail the impacts of chemicals on the human body and the causes of disease. In the mid-1800s, Rudolf Virchow, a German scientist considered to be the founder of pathology (the study of diseased body tissue), began to unlock the mystery of many diseases by studying tissues at the cellular level. His research of diseased cells helped pathologists pinpoint the paths diseases take in the body.

With society's increasing dependence on chemicals (for example, in agriculture, industry, and medicine) and growing use of prescribed

Anthrax Facts and Prevention

Anthrax is an acute infectious disease caused by the spore-forming bacterium *Bacillus anthracis*. This bacteria, when dispersed among large groups of people (such as by mail), can be considered an agent of biological warfare. Infection can occur in three forms: cutaneous (skin), inhalation, and gastrointestinal. However, anthrax antibiotics have been licensed for use in humans. According to the Center for Disease Control and Prevention (CDC), an anthrax vaccine is reported to be 93 percent effective in protecting against the disease.

According to the *Athens Banner-Herald,* though there have been few deaths from anthrax, police, ambulance workers and the mail-receiving public have been on alert as a result of widespread hoaxes. Anthrax hoaxes have been growing for several years, reports the CDC, and reached 300 in 2000.

Here are some tips from the CDC on handling suspect mail:
- Do not open any suspicious mail.
- Keep mail away from your face when you open it.
- Do not blow or sniff mail or mail contents.
- Avoid vigorous handling of mail, such as tearing or shredding.
- Wash your hands after handling the mail.

(and illegal) drugs, the study of the impact of these potential toxins on public health and environmental quality has become more important. The toxicologist's role in determining the extent of a problem, as well as suggesting possible alternatives or antidotes, plays an important role in society. Toxicologists act as consultants on developing long-term solutions to problems such as air and water pollution, the dumping of toxic waste into landfills, and the recognition of an unusual reaction to a pharmaceutical drug.

THE JOB

As scientists, toxicologists are concerned with the detection and effects of toxins, as well as developing methods to treat intoxication (poisonings). A primary objective of a toxicologist is to protect consumers by reducing the risks of accidental exposure to poisons. Toxicologists investigate the many areas in which our society uses potential toxins and documents their impact. For example, a toxicologist may chemically analyze a fish in a local lake to read for mercury, a harmful toxin to humans if consumed in high enough levels.

This reading is reported to government or industry officials, who, in turn, write up a legal policy setting the maximum level of mercury that manufacturing companies can release without contaminating nearby fish and endangering consumers.

On many projects, a toxicologist may be part of a research team, such as at a poison control center or a research laboratory. *Clinical toxicologists* may work to help save emergency drug overdose victims. *Industrial toxicologists* and *academic toxicologists* work on solving long-term issues, such as studying the toxic effects of cigarettes. They may focus on research and development, working to improve and speed up testing methods without sacrificing safety. Toxicologists use the most modern equipment, such as electron microscopes, atomic absorption spectrometers, and mass spectrometers, and they study new research instrumentation that may help with sophisticated research.

Industrial toxicologists work for private companies, testing new products for potential poisons. For example, before a new cosmetic good can be sold, it must be tested according to strict guidelines. Toxicologists oversee this testing, which is often done on laboratory animals. These toxicologists may apply the test article ingredients topically, orally, or by injection. They test the results through observation, blood analysis, and dissection and detailed pathologic examination. Research results are used for labeling and packaging instructions to ensure that customers use the product safely. Although animal experimentation has created a great deal of controversy with animal-rights supporters, humane procedures are stressed throughout toxicology studies.

Toxicologists carefully document their research procedures so that they can be used in later reports on their findings. They often interact with lawyers and legislators on writing legislation. They may also appear at official hearings designed to discuss and implement new policy decisions.

Because toxic materials are often handled during research and experimentation, a toxicologist must pay careful attention to safety procedures.

REQUIREMENTS

High School

While in high school, you can best prepare for a career as a toxicologist by taking courses in both the physical and biological sciences (chemistry and biology, for example), algebra and geometry, and physics. English and other courses that improve written and verbal communication skills will also be useful, since toxicologists must write and report on complicated study results.

Postsecondary Training
Most toxicologists obtain their undergraduate degrees in a scientific field, such as pharmacology or chemistry. Course work should include mathematics (including mathematical modeling), biology, chemistry, statistics, biochemistry, pathology, anatomy, and research methods.

Career opportunities for graduates with bachelor's degrees are limited; the majority of toxicologists go on to obtain master's or doctorate degrees. Graduate programs vary depending on field of study, but they may include courses such as pathology, environmental toxicology, and molecular biology. Doctorate programs generally last four to five years.

Certification or Licensing
Certification reflects an individual's competence and expertise in toxicology and can enhance career opportunities. The American Board of Toxicology certifies toxicologists after they pass a comprehensive two-day examination and complete the necessary educational requirements. To be eligible, applicants with a bachelor's degree in an appropriate field must first have 10 years of work experience; with a master's degree, seven years; and with a doctorate degree, three years.

Other Requirements
Toxicologists must be hard workers and be dedicated to their field of study. To succeed in their work, they must be careful observers and have an eye for detail. Patience is also necessary, since many research projects can last months to years and show little results. The ability to work both alone and as part of a team is also needed for research.

Because of the nature of their work, toxicologists must also realize the potential dangers of working with hazardous materials. They must also be comfortable working with laboratory animals and be able to dissect them to examine organs and tissues. Though efforts have been made to limit and control live animal experimentation, research still requires their use to identify toxins and, in turn, protect the consumer public.

EXPLORING
If you are interested in pursuing a career as a toxicologist, consider joining a science club in addition to taking biology and chemistry

courses to further develop your laboratory skills. Your career counselor might be able to help you arrange a discussion with a practicing toxicologist to explore career options. Part-time jobs in research laboratories or hospitals are an excellent way to explore science firsthand, although opportunities may be limited and require higher levels of education and experience.

EMPLOYERS

According to the Society of Toxicology, approximately 9,000 toxicologists are employed in the United States. A recent job market survey of those with Ph.D.'s shows that 47 percent work for chemical and pharmaceutical companies, 21 percent are employed by large universities or medical schools, and 14 percent work in government. An increasing number (12 percent) work for consulting firms, providing professional recommendations to agencies, industries, and attorneys about issues involving toxic chemicals. Nonprofit research foundations employ only 4 percent of all toxicologists.

STARTING OUT

Those with the necessary education and experience should contact the appropriate research departments in hospitals, colleges and universities, government agencies, or private businesses. Often, school professors and career placement advisors provide job leads and recommendations.

Networking with professionals is another useful way to enter the field. Past work with a team of toxicologists during graduate study may open doors to future research opportunities. Membership in a professional society can also offer more networking contacts. In addition, the Society of Toxicology and the American College of Medical Toxicology both offer job placement assistance to members.

ADVANCEMENT

Skilled toxicologists will find many advancement opportunities, although specific promotions depend on the size and type of organization where the toxicologist is employed. Those working for private companies may become heads of research departments. Because of their involvement in developing important company policy, highly skilled and respected toxicologists may become vice presidents or presidents of companies. Obviously, this type of promotion would entail a change in job responsibilities, involving more administrative tasks than research activities.

Toxicologists working for educational institutions may become professors, heads of a department, or deans. Toxicologists who want to continue to research and teach can advance to positions with higher pay and increased job responsibilities. Toxicologists working at universities usually write grant proposals, teach courses, and train graduate students. University positions often do not pay as well as industrial positions, but they offer more independence in pursuing research interests.

EARNINGS

As trained professionals, toxicologists have good earning potential. Wages vary depending on level of experience, education, and employer. According to the Society of Toxicology, entry-level toxicologists with a Ph.D. earn $35,000 to $60,000. With a Ph.D. and 10 years of experience, they earn between $70,000 and $100,000 a year. Toxicologists in executive positions earn more than $100,000, and in the corporate arena they can earn more than $200,000. Those in private industry earn slightly more than those in government or academic positions.

Salaries for toxicologists are, in general, on the rise, but the survey reports that the biggest factor determining earning potential is not location but type of employer. Certification also plays a large role in salary level; toxicologists who are certified earn higher salaries than those who have not earned certification. Comparing gender differences, the salary survey found that women continue to be paid less than their male counterparts.

WORK ENVIRONMENT

Toxicologists usually work in well-equipped laboratories or offices, either as part of a team or alone. Research in libraries or in the field is a major part of the job. Some toxicologists work a standard 40-hour workweek, although many work longer hours. Overtime should be expected if an important research project is on deadline. Research and experimentation can be both physically and mentally tiring, with much of the laboratory work and analysis done while under time restrictions. Some travel may be required to testify at hearings, to collect field samples, or to attend professional conferences.

Toxicologists often work on research that has important health considerations. At a poison control center, for example, toxicologists may try to find information about the poisonous properties of a product while an overdose victim's life is in danger. Because their work involves studying the impact of toxic material, toxicologists must be willing to handle contaminated material and adhere to the strict safety precautions required.

OUTLOOK

Employment opportunities for toxicologists are expected to continue to be good. The growing use of chemicals and pharmaceuticals by society has created demand for trained professionals to determine and limit the health risks associated with potential toxins. In addition, new concerns over bioterrorism and the potential use of chemical weapons will create more demand for toxicologists to help develop new vaccines and other antibiotics. However, according to the Society of Toxicology, the job market for toxicologists, especially in traditional fields, is still expected to be tight.

Job opportunities should be greatest in large urban areas where many large hospitals, chemical manufacturers, and university research facilities are located. Those with the most training and experience will have the best employment prospects.

FOR MORE INFORMATION

For certification information, contact
American Board of Toxicology
PO Box 30054
Raleigh, NC 27622
Tel: 919-572-5525
Email: abtox@mindspring.com
http://www.abtox.org

For information on educational programs and other toxicology resources, contact
American College of Medical Toxicology
11240 Waples Mill Road, Suite 200
Farifax, VA 22030
Email: info@acmt.net
Tel: 703-934-1223
http://www.acmt.net

For general career information, contact
Society of Toxicology
1821 Michael Faraday Drive, Suite 300
Reston, VA 20190
Tel: 703-438-3115
Email: sothq@toxicology.org
http://www.toxicology.org

Veterinarians

School Subjects
Biology
Chemistry

Personal Skills
Helping/teaching
Technical/scientific

Work Environment
Primarily indoors
Primarily one location

Minimum Education Level
Medical degree

Salary Range
$38,400 to $64,750 to
$123,040+

Certification or Licensing
Required

Outlook
Faster than the average

DOT
073

GOE
02.02.01

NOC
3114

O*NET-SOC
29-1131.00

OVERVIEW

The *veterinarian,* or *doctor of veterinary medicine,* diagnoses and controls animal diseases, treats sick and injured animals medically and surgically, prevents transmission of animal diseases, and advises owners on proper care of pets and livestock. Veterinarians are dedicated to the protection of the health and welfare of all animals and to society as a whole. There are about 58,000 veterinarians in the United States.

HISTORY

The first school of veterinary medicine was opened in 1762 at Lyons, France, and it was a French immigrant who established the practice of veterinary medicine in the United States 100 years later. Veterinary medicine has made great strides since its introduction in this country, one advance being the significant reduction in animal diseases contracted by humans.

THE JOB

Veterinarians ensure a safe food supply by maintaining the health of food animals. They also protect the public from residues of herbicides, pesticides, and antibiotics in food. Veterinarians may be involved in wildlife preservation and conservation and use their knowledge to increase food production through genetics, animal feed production, and preventive medicine.

In North America, about 70 percent of veterinarians are employees of established veterinary practices. Although some veterinarians treat all kinds of animals, more than half limit their practice to companion animals such as dogs, cats, and birds. A smaller number of veterinarians work mainly with horses, cattle, pigs, sheep, goats, and poultry. Today, a veterinarian may be treating llamas, catfish, or ostriches as well. Others are employed by wildlife management groups, zoos, aquariums, ranches, feed lots, fish farms, and animal shelters.

Veterinarians in private practice diagnose and treat animal health problems. During yearly checkups, the veterinarian records the animal's temperature and weight; inspects its mouth, eyes, and ears; inspects the skin or coat for any signs of abnormalities; observes any peculiarities in the animal's behavior; and discusses the animals eating, sleeping, and exercise habits at length with the owner. The veterinarian will also check the animal's vaccination records and administer inoculations for rabies, distemper, and other diseases if necessary. If the veterinarian or owner notes any special concerns, or if the animal is taken to the veterinarian for a specific procedure, such as spaying or neutering, dental cleaning, or setting broken bones, the animal may stay at the veterinarian's office for one or several days for surgery, observation, or extended treatments. If a sick or wounded animal is beyond medical help, the veterinarian may, with the consent of the owner, have to euthanize the animal.

During office visits and surgery, veterinarians use traditional medical instruments, such as stethoscopes, thermometers, and surgical instruments, and standard tests, such as X rays and diagnostic medical sonography, to evaluate the animal's health. Veterinarians may also prescribe drugs for the animal, which the owner purchases at the veterinarian's office.

Some veterinarians work in public and corporate sectors. Many are employed by city, county, state, provincial, or federal government agencies that investigate, test for, and control diseases in companion animals, livestock, and poultry that affect both animal and human health. Veterinarians also play an important public health role. For example, veterinarians played an important part in conquering diseases such as malaria and yellow fever.

Pharmaceutical and biomedical research firms hire veterinarians to develop, test, and supervise the production of drugs, chemicals, and biological products such as antibiotics and vaccines that are designed for human and animal use. Some veterinarians are employed in management, technical sales and services, and marketing in agribusiness, pet food companies, and pharmaceutical companies. Still other veterinarians are engaged in research and teaching at veterinary and human medical schools, working with racetracks or animal-related enterprises, or working within the military, public health corps, and space agencies.

Salary Disparities

According to the business consulting group KPMG, pay for veterinarians lags far behind the pay of other medical professionals. Thirty years ago, salaries were closer to the same level; today, vets earn approximately $70,000 to $80,000 a year while physicians earn more than twice that amount.

Veterinarians in private clinical practice become specialists in surgery, anesthesiology, dentistry, internal medicine, ophthalmology, or radiology. Many veterinarians also pursue advanced degrees in the basic sciences, such as anatomy, microbiology, and physiology. Veterinarians who seek specialty board certification in one of 20 specialty fields must complete a two- to five-year residency program and must pass an additional examination. Some veterinarians combine their degree in veterinary medicine with a degree in business (M.B.A.) or law (J.D.).

The U.S. Department of Agriculture has opportunities for veterinarians in the food safety inspection service and the animal and plant health inspection service, notably in the areas of food hygiene and safety, animal welfare, animal disease control, and research. Agencies in the U.S. Department of Agriculture utilize veterinarians in positions related to research on diseases transmissible from animals to human beings and on the acceptance and use of drugs for treatment or prevention of diseases. Veterinarians also are employed by the Environmental Protection Agency to deal with public health and environmental risks to the human population.

Veterinarians are often assisted by *veterinary technicians,* who may conduct basic tests, record an animal's medical history for the veterinarian's review, and assist the veterinarian in surgical procedures.

REQUIREMENTS
High School
For the high school student who is interested in admission to a school of veterinary medicine, a college preparatory course is a wise choice. A strong emphasis on science classes such as biology, chemistry, and anatomy is highly recommended.

Postsecondary Training
The doctor of veterinary medicine (D.V.M.) degree requires a minimum of four years of study at an accredited college of veterinary med-

icine. Although many of these colleges do not require a bachelor's degree for admission, most require applicants to have completed 45–90 hours of undergraduate study. It is possible to obtain preveterinary training in a junior college, but since admission to colleges of veterinary medicine is an extremely competitive process, most students receive degrees from four-year colleges before applying. In addition to academic instruction, veterinary education includes clinical experience in diagnosing disease and treating animals, performing surgery, and performing laboratory work in anatomy, biochemistry, and other scientific and medical subjects.

There are 28 colleges of veterinary medicine in the United States that are accredited by the Council of Veterinary Medicine of the American Veterinary Medical Association. Each college of veterinary medicine has its own preveterinary requirements, which typically include basic language arts, social sciences, humanities, mathematics, chemistry, and biological and physical sciences.

Applicants to schools of veterinary medicine usually must have grades of "B" or better, especially in the sciences. Applicants must take the Veterinary Aptitude Test, Medical College Admission Test, or the Graduate Record Examination. Fewer than half of the applicants to schools of veterinary medicine may be admitted, due to small class sizes and limited facilities. Most colleges give preference to candidates with animal- or veterinary-related experience. Colleges usually give preference to in-state applicants because most colleges of veterinary medicine are state-supported. There are regional agreements in which states without veterinary schools send students to designated regional schools.

Certification or Licensing

All states and the District of Columbia require that veterinarians be licensed to practice private clinical medicine. To obtain a license, applicants must have a D.V.M. degree from an accredited or approved college of veterinary medicine. They must also pass one or more national examinations and an examination in the state in which they plan to practice.

Few states issue licenses to veterinarians already licensed by another state. Thus, if a veterinarian moves from one state to another, he or she will probably have to go through the licensing process again. Approximately half of the states require veterinarians to attend continuing education courses in order to maintain their licenses. Veterinarians may be employed by a government agency (such as the U.S. Department of Agriculture) or at some academic institution without having a state license.

Other Requirements

Individuals who are interested in veterinary medicine should have an inquiring mind and keen powers of observation. Aptitude and interest in the biological sciences are important. Veterinarians need a lifelong interest in scientific learning as well as a liking and understanding of animals. Veterinarians should be able to meet, talk, and work well with a variety of people. An ability to communicate with the animal owner is as important in a veterinarian as diagnostic skills.

Veterinarians use state-of-the-art medical equipment, such as electron microscopes, laser surgery, radiation therapy, and ultrasound, to diagnose animal diseases and to treat sick or injured animals. Although manual dexterity and physical stamina are often required, especially for farm vets, important roles in veterinary medicine can be adapted for those with disabilities.

Interaction with animal owners is an very important part of being a veterinarian. The discussions between vet and owner are critical to the veterinarian's diagnosis, so he or she must be able to communicate effectively and get along with a wide variety of personalities. Veterinarians may have to euthanize (that is, humanely kill) an animal that is very sick or severely injured and cannot get well. When a beloved pet dies, the veterinarian must deal with the owner's grief and loss.

EXPLORING

High school students interested in becoming veterinarians may find part-time or volunteer work on farms, in small-animal clinics, or in pet shops, animal shelters, or research laboratories. Participation in extracurricular activities such as 4-H are good ways to learn about the care of animals. Such experience is important because, as already noted, many schools of veterinary medicine have established experience with animals as a criterion for admission to their programs.

EMPLOYERS

Veterinarians may be employed by the government, schools and universities, wildlife management groups, zoos, aquariums, ranches, feed lots, fish farms, or pet food or pharmaceutical companies. The vast majority, however, are employed by veterinary clinical practices or hospitals. Many successful veterinarians in private practice are self-employed and may even employ other veterinarians. An increase in the demand for veterinarians is anticipated, particularly for those who specialize in areas related to public health issues such as food safety

Petey the cat is examined by a veterinarian during an annual check-up. *(Richard Hutchings/Photo Researchers, Inc.)*

and disease control. Cities and large metropolitan areas will probably provide the bulk of new jobs for these specialists, while jobs for veterinarians who specialize in large animals will be focused in rural, remote areas.

STARTING OUT

The only way to become a veterinarian is through the prescribed degree program, and vet schools are set up to assist their graduates in finding employment. Veterinarians who wish to enter private clinical practice must have a license to practice in their particular state before opening an office. Licenses are obtained by passing the state's examination.

ADVANCEMENT

New graduate veterinarians may enter private clinical practice, usually as employees in an established practice, or become employees of the U.S. government as meat and poultry inspectors, disease control workers, and commissioned officers in the U.S. Public Health Service or the military. New graduates may also enter internships and residencies at veterinary colleges and large private and public veterinary practices or become employed by industrial firms.

The veterinarian who is employed by a government agency may advance in grade and salary after accumulating time and experience on the job. For the veterinarian in private clinical practice, advancement usually consists of an expanding practice and the higher income that will result from it or becoming an owner of several practices.

Those who teach or do research may obtain a doctorate and move from the rank of instructor to that of full professor, or they may advance to an administrative position.

EARNINGS

The U.S. Department of Labor reports that median annual earnings of veterinarians were $64,750 in 2003. Salaries ranged from less than $38,400 to more than $123,040. The average annual salary for veterinarians working for the federal government was $72,208 in 2003.

According to a survey by the American Veterinary Medical Association, the average starting salary for veterinary medical college graduates who worked exclusively with small animals was $48,178 in 2002. Those who worked exclusively with large animals earned an average of $48,303. Equine veterinarians earned an average of $34,273 to start.

WORK ENVIRONMENT

Veterinarians usually treat companion and food animals in hospitals and clinics. Those in large animal practice also work out of well-equipped trucks or cars and may drive considerable distances to farms and ranches. They may work outdoors in all kinds of weather. The chief risk for veterinarians is injury by animals; however, modern tranquilizers and technology have made it much easier to work on all types of animals.

Most veterinarians work long hours, often 50 or more hours a week. Although those in private clinical practice may work nights and weekends, the increased number of emergency clinics has reduced the amount of time private practitioners have to be on call. Large animal practitioners tend to work more irregular hours than those in small animal practice, industry, or government. Veterinarians who are just starting a practice tend to work longer hours.

OUTLOOK

Employment of veterinarians is expected to grow faster than the average through 2012. The number of pets is expected to increase slightly because of rising incomes and an increase in the number of people aged 34 to 59, among whom pet ownership has been highest in the past. Many single adults and senior citizens have come to appreciate animal ownership. Pet owners also may be willing to pay for more elective and intensive care than in the past. In addition, emphasis on scientific methods of breeding and raising livestock, poultry, and fish and continued support for public health and disease control programs will contribute to the demand for veterinarians. The number of jobs stemming from the need to replace workers will be equal to new job growth.

The outlook is good for veterinarians with specialty training. Demand for specialists in toxicology, laboratory animal medicine, and pathology is expected to increase. Most jobs for specialists will be in metropolitan areas. Prospects for veterinarians who concentrate on environmental and public health issues, aquaculture, and food animal practice appear to be excellent because of perceived increased need in these areas. Positions in small animal specialties will be competitive. Opportunities in farm animal specialties will be better, since most such positions are located in remote, rural areas.

Despite the availability of additional jobs, competition among veterinarians is likely to be stiff. First-year enrollments in veterinary schools have increased slightly, and the number of students in graduate-degree and board-certification programs has risen dramatically.

FOR MORE INFORMATION

For more information on careers, schools, and resources, contact
American Veterinary Medical Association
1931 North Meacham Road, Suite 100
Schaumburg, IL 60173-4360
Attn: Education and Research Division
Tel: 847-925-8070
Email: avmainfo@avma.org
http://www.avma.org

For information on veterinary opportunities in the federal government, contact
Animal and Plant Health Inspection Service
U.S. Department of Agriculture
12th and Independence Avenue, SW
Washington, DC 20250
Email: APHIS.Web@aphis.usda.gov
http://www.aphis.usda.gov

The following website offers links to educational and career resources for veterinarians.

NetVet
http://netvet.wustl.edu/vet.htm

Zoologists

OVERVIEW

Zoologists are biologists who study animals. They often select a particular type of animal to study, and they may study an entire animal, one part or aspect of an animal, or a whole animal society. There are many areas of specialization from which a zoologist can choose, such as origins, genetics, characteristics, classifications, behaviors, life processes, and distribution of animals.

HISTORY

Human beings have always studied animals. Knowledge of animal behavior was a necessity to prehistoric humans, whose survival depended on their success in hunting. Those early people who hunted to live learned to respect and even revere their prey. The earliest known paintings, located in the Lascaux Caves in France, depict animals, which demonstrates the importance of animals to early humans. Most experts believe that the artists who painted those images viewed the animals they hunted not just as a food source, but also as an important element of spiritual or religious life.

The first important developments in zoology occurred in Greece, where Alcmaeon, a philosopher and physician, studied animals and performed the first known dissections of humans in the sixth century B.C. Aristotle, however, is generally considered to be the first real zoologist. Aristotle, who studied with the great philosopher Plato and tutored the world-conquering Alexander the Great, had the lofty goal of setting down in writing everything that was known in his time. In an attempt to extend that knowledge, he observed and dissected sea creatures. He also devised a system of classifying animals that included 500 species, a system that influenced scientists for many centuries after his death. Some scholars believe that Alexander sent various exotic animals to his old tutor from the lands he conquered, giving Aristotle unparalleled access to the animals of the ancient world.

With the exception of important work in physiology done by the Roman physician Galen, the study of zoology progressed little after Aristotle until the middle of the 16th century. Between 1555 and 1700, much significant work was done in the classification of species and in physiology, especially regarding the circulation of blood, which affected studies of both animals and humans. The invention of the microscope in approximately 1590 led to the discovery and study of cells. In the 18th century, Swedish botanist Carl Linnaeus developed the system of classification of plants and animals that is still used.

Zoology continued to develop at a rapid rate, and in 1859, Charles Darwin published *On the Origin of Species,* which promoted the theory of natural selection, revolutionized the way scientists viewed all living creatures, and gave rise to the field of ethology, the study of animal behavior. Since that time, zoologists throughout the world have made innumerable advances.

In the past century, the rapid development of technology has changed zoology and all sciences by giving scientists the tools to explore areas that had previously been closed to them. Computers, submersibles, spacecraft, and tremendously powerful microscopes are only a few of the means that modern zoologists have used to bring new knowledge to light. In spite of these advances, however, mysteries remain, questions go unanswered, and species wait to be discovered.

THE JOB

Although zoology is a single specialty within the field of biology, it is a vast specialty that includes many major subspecialties. Some zoologists study a single animal or a category of animals, whereas others may specialize in a particular part of an animal's anatomy or study a process that takes place in many kinds of animals. A zoologist might study single-cell organisms, a particular variety of fish, or the behavior of groups of animals such as elephants or bees.

Many zoologists are classified according to the animals they study. For example, *entomologists* are experts on insects, *ichthyologists* study fish, *herpetologists* specialize in the study of reptiles and amphibians, *mammalogists* focus on mammals, and *ornithologists* study birds. *Embryologists,* however, are classified according to the process that they study. They examine the ways in which animal embryos form and develop from conception to birth.

Within each primary area of specialization there is a wide range of subspecialties. An ichthyologist, for example, might focus on the physiology, or physical structure and functioning, of a particular fish; on a biochemical phenomenon such as bioluminescence in deep-sea species; on the discovery and classification of fish; on variations within a single species in different parts of the world; or on the ways in which one type of fish interacts with other species in a specific environment. Others may specialize in the effects of pollution on fish or in finding ways to grow fish effectively in controlled environments in order to increase the supply of healthy food available for human consumption.

Some zoologists are primarily teachers, while others spend most of their time performing original research. Teaching jobs in universities and other facilities are probably the most secure positions available, but zoologists who wish to do extensive research may find such positions restrictive. Even zoologists whose primary function is research, however, often need to do some teaching in the course of their work, and almost everyone in the field has to deal with the public at one time or another. As Dr. R. Grant Gilmore, a fish ecologist who is a senior scientist and former director of marine science at the Harbor Branch Oceanographic Institute, says, "In marine science, it's a public day, too. You do get reporters calling about odd things all the time. That happens. People don't realize that, but you end up going before the public eye whether you want to or not."

Students often believe that zoological scientists spend most of their time in the field, observing animals and collecting specimens. In fact, most researchers spend no more than two to eight weeks in the field each year. Zoologists spend much of their time at a computer or on the telephone. Speaking of his daily activities, Dr. Gilmore says, "Getting up and starting with correspondence is, I think, number one. We communicate with colleagues all the time, and with the young people wanting to get into the field, and that's one thing we try to get out right away. We try to get letters and telephone calls returned. That's another thing. I think most people think they're going to be out in the boat, diving. No. You communicate. You communicate with the granting agencies, people that are going to support you. You communicate with the people that are going to work for you, or students. There's an awful lot of that going on. Part of my day, two or three hours, is devoted to that, and that alone. And then it's a joy to get to your data."

It is often the case that junior scientists spend more time in the field than do senior scientists, who study specimens and data collected in the field by their younger colleagues. Senior scientists spend much of their time coordinating research, directing younger scientists and technicians, and writing grant proposals or soliciting funds in other ways.

Raising money is an extremely important activity for zoologists who are not employed by government agencies or major universities. The process of obtaining money for research can be time consuming and difficult. Dr. Gilmore, an expert fund-raiser, views it as the most difficult part of his job. Good development skills can also give scientists a flexibility that government-funded scientists do not have. Government money is sometimes available only for research in narrowly defined areas that may not be those that a scientist wishes to study. A zoologist who wants to study a particular area may seek his or her own funding in order not to be limited by government restrictions.

REQUIREMENTS

High School

To prepare for a career in zoology, make sure to get a well-rounded high school education. Although a solid grounding in biology and chemistry is an absolute necessity, you should remember that facility in English will also be invaluable. Writing monographs and articles, communicating with colleagues both orally and in writing, and writing persuasive fund-raising proposals are all activities at which scientists need to excel. You should also read widely, not merely relying on books on science or other subjects that are required by the school. The scientist-in-training should search the library for magazines and journals dealing with areas that are of personal interest. Developing the habit of reading will help prepare you for the massive amounts of reading involved in research and keeping up with the latest developments in the field. Computer skills are also essential, since most zoologists not only use the computer for writing, communication, and research, but they also use various software packages to perform statistical analyses.

Postsecondary Training

Dr. R. Grant Gilmore recommends that college students who are interested in zoology avoid specializing at the undergraduate level. "I would say the best bet is to get a good liberal arts degree and emphasize the sciences. If you're interested in biology, emphasize the biological sciences. And then, your graduate level is when you really make up your mind which direction you're going to go. But if you have the aptitude for the sciences, I think you should try a number of the different sciences. Just play the field when you can," he says.

A bachelor's degree is the minimum requirement to work as a zoologist; advanced degrees are needed for research or administrative work. Academic training, practical experience, and the ability to work effectively with others are the most important prerequisites for a career in zoology.

Other Requirements

Success in zoology requires tremendous effort. It would be unwise for a person who wants to work an eight-hour day to become a zoologist, since hard work and long hours (sometimes 60 to 80 hours per week) are the norm. Also, although some top scientists are paid extremely well, the field does not provide a rapid route to riches. A successful zoologist finds satisfaction in work, not in a paycheck. The personal rewards, however, can be tremendous. The typical zoologist finds his or her work satisfying on many levels.

A successful zoologist is generally patient and flexible. A person who cannot juggle various tasks will have a difficult time in a job that requires doing research, writing articles, dealing with the public, teaching students, soliciting funds, and keeping up with the latest publications in the field. Flexibility also comes into play when funding for a particular area of study ends or is unavailable. A zoologist whose range of expertise is too narrowly focused will be at a disadvantage when there are no opportunities in that particular area. A flexible approach and a willingness to explore various areas can be crucial in such situations, and a too-rigid attitude may lead a zoologist to avoid studies that he or she would have found rewarding.

An aptitude for reading and writing is a must for any zoologist. A person who hates to read would have difficulty keeping up with the literature in the field, and a person who cannot write or dislikes writing would be unable to write effective articles and books. Publishing is an important part of zoological work, especially for those who are conducting research.

EXPLORING

One of the best ways to find out if you are suited for a career as a zoologist is to talk to zoologists and find out exactly what they do. Contact experts in your field of interest. If you are interested in birds, find out whether there is an ornithologist in your area. If there is not, find an expert in some other part of the country. Read books, magazines, and journals to find out who the experts are. Don't be afraid to write or call people and ask them questions.

One good way to meet experts is to attend meetings of professional organizations. If you are interested in fish, locate organizations of ichthyologists by searching in the library or on the Internet. If you can, attend an organization's meeting and introduce yourself to the attendees. Ask questions and learn as much as you can.

Try to become an intern or a volunteer at an organization that is involved in an area that you find interesting. Most organizations have internships, and if you look with determination for an internship, you are likely to find one.

EMPLOYERS

Zoologists are employed by a wide variety of institutions, not just zoos. Many zoologists are teachers at universities and other facilities, where they may teach during the year while spending their summers doing research. A large number of zoologists are researchers; they may be working for nonprofit organizations (requiring grants to fund their work), scientific institutions, or the government. Of course, there are many zoologists who are employed by zoos, aquariums, and museums. While jobs for zoologists exist all over the country, large cities that have universities, zoos, and museums will provide far more opportunities for zoologists than in rural areas.

STARTING OUT

Though it is possible to find work with a bachelor's degree, it is likely that you will need to continue your education to advance further in the field. Competition for higher paying, high-level jobs among those with doctoral degrees is fierce; as a result, it is often easier to break into the field with a master's degree than it is with a Ph.D. Many zoologists with their master's degree seek a mid-level job and work toward a Ph.D. on a part-time basis.

According to Dr. R. Grant Gilmore, the best way to get your first job in zoology is through people you know. "Make as many personal contacts as possible. And try to get a qualified scientist to help you; someone who really knows the field and knows other people. If your adviser doesn't, try to find one who does," he says. "It's so competitive right now that the personal contact really makes a difference."

You will be ahead of the game if you have made contacts as an intern or as a member of a professional organization. It is an excellent idea to attend the meetings of professional organizations, which generally welcome students. At those meetings, introduce yourself to the scientists you admire and ask for their help and advice. Gilmore says, "I see too many students these days hesitating to go up to that renowned scientist and talk to him. Just go up and carry on a conversation. They seem to be afraid to do that. I think that's a big mistake."

Don't be shy, but be sure to treat people with respect. Ultimately, it's the way you relate to other people that determines how your career will develop. Says Gilmore, "I don't care what GPA you have. I don't care what SAT score you have or GRE score you have. That does not make one bit of difference. Everybody has high scores these days. It's the way you present yourself, your interests, the way you act. And that personal contact that makes all the difference."

ADVANCEMENT

Higher education and publishing are two of the most important means of advancing in the field of zoology. The holder of a Ph.D. will make more money and have a higher status than the holder of a bachelor's or master's degree. The publication of articles and books is important for both research scientists and professors of zoology. A young professor who does not publish cannot expect to become a full professor with tenure, and a research scientist who does not publish the results of his or her research will not become known as an authority in the field. In addition, the publication of a significant work lets everyone in the field know that the author has worked hard and accomplished something worthwhile.

Because zoology is not a career in which people typically move from job to job, people generally move up within an organization. A professor may become a full professor; a research scientist may become known as an expert in the field or may become the head of a department, division, or institution; a zoologist employed by an aquarium or a zoo may become an administrator or head curator. In some cases, however, scientists may not want what appears to be a more prestigious position. A zoologist who loves to conduct and coordinate research, for example, may not want to become an administrator who is responsible for budgeting, hiring and firing, and other tasks that have nothing to do with research.

EARNINGS

A study conducted by the National Association of Colleges and Employers determined that in 2003 beginning salaries averaged

$29,456 for holders of bachelor's degrees in biological science (including zoologists), $33,600 for those with master's degrees, and $42,244 for holders of doctoral degrees.

According to the U.S. Department of Labor, the median annual wage for biological scientists in 2003 was $49,330. Salaries ranged from less than $30,000 a year to more than $75,000 a year, depending on the zoologist's education and experience.

The benefits that zoologists receive as part of their employment vary widely. Employees of the federal government or top universities tend to have extensive benefit packages, but the benefits offered by private industry cover a wide range, from extremely generous to almost nonexistent.

WORK ENVIRONMENT

There is much variation in the conditions under which zoologists work. Professors of zoology may teach exclusively during the school year or may both teach and conduct research. Many professors whose school year consists of teaching spend their summers doing research. Research scientists spend some time in the field, but most of their work is done in the laboratory. There are zoologists who spend most of their time in the field, but they are the exceptions to the rule.

Zoologists who do field work may have to deal with difficult conditions. A gorilla expert may have to spend her time in the forests of Rwanda; a shark expert may need to observe his subjects from a shark cage. For most people in the field, however, that aspect of the work is particularly interesting and satisfying.

Zoologists spend much of their time corresponding with others in their field, studying the latest literature, reviewing articles written by their peers, and making and returning phone calls. They also log many hours working with computers, using computer modeling, performing statistical analyses, recording the results of their research, or writing articles and grant proposals.

No zoologist works in a vacuum. Even those who spend much time in the field have to keep up with developments within their specialty. In most cases, zoologists deal with many different kinds of people, including students, mentors, the public, colleagues, representatives of granting agencies, private or corporate donors, reporters, and science writers. For this reason, the most successful members of the profession tend to develop good communication skills.

OUTLOOK

According to the *Occupational Outlook Handbook*, job opportunities for biological scientists should grow at an average rate through 2012. Competition for good positions—especially research positions that require a Ph.D.—is high.

Those with a bachelor's or master's degree will face less competition due to a larger number of available positions, especially in nonresearch areas. Growth in the biological sciences should continue to increase in the next decade, spurred partly by the need to analyze and offset the effects of pollution on the environment.

Those who are most successful in the field in the future are likely to be those who are able to diversify. Dr. R. Grant Gilmore, who believes that the need for well-trained zoologists will increase in the next century, advises those entering the field to stay open-minded, maintain a wide range of contacts, and keep an eye out for what is occurring in related fields. "There is a danger in science today. People become so narrowly focused that it endangers their future. There's an ecological concept which I like to use that says 'Diversity is stability.' If you put all your marbles in one basket and somebody tips that basket, you're done for. Keep an open mind and keep open contacts."

FOR MORE INFORMATION

For information on careers, schools, internships, and job opportunities, check out the following websites or contact

American Association of Zoo Keepers
3601 Southwest 29th Street, Suite 133
Topeka, KS 66614
http://www.aazk.org

American Institute of Biological Sciences
1444 Eye Street, NW, Suite 200
Washington, DC 20005
Tel: 202-628-1500
http://www.aibs.org

American Zoo and Aquarium Association
8403 Colesville Road, Suite 710
Silver Spring, MD 20910-3314
Tel: 301-562-0777
Email: generalinquiry@aza.org
http://www.aza.org

The following society publishes the bimonthly journal Integrative and Comparative Biology, *and it is a good source of information about all areas and aspects of zoology. For more information, contact*

Society for Integrative and Comparative Biology
1313 Dolley Madison Boulevard, Suite 402
McLean, VA 22101
Tel: 800-955-1236
http://www.sicb.org

Index

Entries and page numbers in **bold** indicate major treatment of a topic.